Access 95
one step at a time

BOOKS AVAILABLE

By both authors:

BP294 A Concise Introduction to Microsoft Works
BP306 A Concise Introduction to Ami Pro 3
BP319 Making MS-DOS work for you
BP327 DOS one step at a time
BP336 A Concise User's Guide to Lotus 1-2-3 Release 3.4
BP337 A Concise User's Guide to Lotus 1-2-3 for Windows
BP341 MS-DOS 6 explained
BP343 A concise introd'n to Microsoft Works for Windows
BP346 Programming in Visual Basic for Windows
BP351 WordPerfect 6 explained
BP352 Excel 5 explained
BP353 WordPerfect 6.0 for Windows explained
BP354 Word 6 for Windows explained
BP362 Access one step at a time
BP372 CA-SuperCalc for Windows explained
BP387 Windows one step at a time*
BP388 Why not personalise your PC
BP399 Windows 95 one step at a time*
BP400 Windows 95 explained
BP402 MS Office one step at a time
BP405 MS Works for Windows 95 explained
BP406 Word 95 explained
BP407 Excel 95 explained
BP408 Access 95 one step at a time
BP409 MS Office 95 one step at a time

By Noel Kantaris:

BP232 A Concise Introduction to MS-DOS
BP250 Programming in FORTRAN 77
BP258 Learning to Program in C
BP259 A Concise Introduction to UNIX*
BP261 A Concise Introduction to Lotus 1-2-3
BP264 A Concise Advanced User's Guide to MS-DOS
BP274 A Concise Introduction to SuperCalc 5
BP284 Programming in QuickBASIC
BP314 A Concise Introduction to Quattro Pro 3.0
BP325 A Concise User's Guide to Windows 3.1
BP330 A Concise User's Guide to Lotus 1-2-3 Release 2.4

Access 95
one step at a time

by

N. Kantaris
and
P.R.M. Oliver

BERNARD BABANI (publishing) LTD.
THE GRAMPIANS
SHEPHERDS BUSH ROAD
LONDON W6 7NF
ENGLAND

PLEASE NOTE

Although every care has been taken with the production of this book to ensure that any projects, designs, modifications and/or programs, etc., contained herewith, operate in a correct and safe manner and also that any components specified are normally available in Great Britain, the Publishers and Author(s) do not accept responsibility in any way for the failure (including fault in design) of any project, design, modification or program to work correctly or to cause damage to any equipment that it may be connected to or used in conjunction with, or in respect of any other damage or injury that may be so caused, nor do the Publishers accept responsibility in any way for the failure to obtain specified components.

Notice is also given that if equipment that is still under warranty is modified in any way or used or connected with home-built equipment then that warranty may be void.

First Published - June 1996

British Library Cataloguing in Publication Data:

A catalogue record for this book is available from the
British Library

ISBN 0 85934 408 8

Cover Design by Gregor Arthur
Cover illustration by Adam Willis
Printed and Bound in Great Britain by Cox & Wyman Ltd, Reading

ABOUT THIS BOOK

Access 95 one step at a time has been written to help users to store and retrieve information using this latest Windows database from Microsoft. No previous knowledge of database design is assumed.

The book does not describe how to install Microsoft Windows 95, or how to set up your computer's hardware. If you need to know more about these topics, then may we suggest that you select an appropriate level book for your needs from the 'Books Available' list - the books are graduated in complexity with the less demanding *One step at a time* series, followed by the *Concise Introduction* series, to the more detailed *Explained* series. They are all published by BERNARD BABANI (publishing) Ltd.

In the first chapter, we give an overview of the database systems and we define the elements that make up an Access relational database management system. The hardware and software requirements of your system are also discussed, so that you know in advance the minimum system configuration for the successful installation and use of the package.

Below we list the major enhancements found in this latest version of Microsoft Access for Windows 95 over the previous version. These are:

- Revamped online help system and extended IntelliSense technology.

- New and improved Wizards making it easy to create and maintain a number of common business and personal databases. There are Wizards to create your tables, forms and reports.

- The ability to import data into Access quickly and easily from other databases.

- The ability to reorganise imported data into tables for maximum efficiency.

- The ability to share work with others across a network.

- The ability to find information in a database with just a few mouse clicks.

- The ability to quickly format forms and reports in a consistent style.

- The ability to automate repetitive tasks and create custom applications with the use of Visual Basic.

- The ability to use Access with Excel for Windows 95 to manage your data effectively.

Most features of the package (old and new) will be discussed using simple examples that the user is encouraged to type in, save, and modify as more advanced features are introduced. This provides the new user with an example that aims to help with the learning of the most commonly used features of the package, and should help to provide the confidence needed to tackle some of the more advanced features later.

This book was written with the busy person in mind. It is not necessary to learn all there is to know about a subject, when reading a few selected pages can usually do the same thing quite adequately!

With the help of this book, it is hoped that you will be able to come to terms with Microsoft Access and get the most out of your computer in terms of efficiency, productivity and enjoyment, and that you will be able to do it in the shortest, most effective and informative way.

ABOUT THE AUTHORS

Noel Kantaris graduated in Electrical Engineering at Bristol University and after spending three years in the Electronics Industry in London, took up a Tutorship in Physics at the University of Queensland. Research interests in Ionospheric Physics, led to the degrees of M.E. in Electronics and Ph.D. in Physics. On return to the UK, he took up a Post-Doctoral Research Fellowship in Radio Physics at the University of Leicester, and then in 1973 a lecturing position in Engineering at the Camborne School of Mines, Cornwall, (part of Exeter University), where since 1978 he has also assumed the responsibility for the Computing Department.

Phil Oliver graduated in Mining Engineering at Camborne School of Mines in 1967 and since then has specialised in most aspects of surface mining technology, with a particular emphasis on computer related techniques. He has worked in Guyana, Canada, several Middle Eastern countries, South Africa and the United Kingdom, on such diverse projects as: the planning and management of bauxite, iron, gold and coal mines; rock excavation contracting in the UK; international mining equipment sales and international mine consulting for a major mining house in South Africa. In 1988 he took up a lecturing position at Camborne School of Mines (part of Exeter University) in Surface Mining and Management.

ACKNOWLEDGEMENTS

We would like to thank the staff of Text 100 Limited for providing the software programs on which this work was based. We would also like to thank colleagues at the Camborne School of Mines for the helpful tips and suggestions which assisted us in the writing of this book.

TRADEMARKS

CONTENTS

1. **PACKAGE OVERVIEW** 1

Hardware and Software Requirements 3
Installing Access 4
The Office Shortcut Bar 6

2. **STARTING ACCESS** 7

Parts of the Access Screen 8
The Menu Bar Options 11
The Mouse Pointers 14
Shortcut Menus 16
Using Help in Access 17

3. **DATABASE BASICS** 19

Database Elements 19
Designing a Database Table 21
    Redesigning a Database Table 23
Sorting a Database Table 25
    Applying a Filter to a Sort 26
Using a Database Form 27
Working with Data 28
    Printing a Table View 30

4. **RELATIONAL DATABASE DESIGN** 31

Relationships 35
Viewing and Editing Relationships 37
Creating an Additional Table 39

5. **CREATING A QUERY** 41

Types of Queries 43
The Query Window 44
    Creating a New Query 45
    Adding Fields to a Query Window 46
Types of Criteria 48
    Using Wildcard Characters in Criteria 48
Combining Criteria 49
Creating Calculated Fields 52

Using Functions in Criteria 54
    Finding Part of a Text Field 54
    Finding Part of a Data Field 55
    Calculating Totals in Queries 55

6.   ADVANCED QUERIES 57

Types of Joins 59
Using a Parameter Query 60
Creating a Crosstab Query 62
Creating Queries for Updating Records 65
Creating Action Queries 66

7.   USING FORMS & REPORTS 71

Using the Form Wizard 72
Customising a Form 76
The Toolbox 78
Using the Report Wizard 82

8. MASKING AND FILTERING DATA 85

The InputMask Property 85
Importing or Linking Data 90
Converting Data to Microsoft Access 93
    The Table Analyzer Wizard 97
    Rebuilding Formulae to Calculate Values . 100

GLOSSARY OF TERMS 103

INDEX 111

1. PACKAGE OVERVIEW

Microsoft Access is a database management system (DBMS) designed to allow users to store, manipulate and retrieve information easily and quickly. A database is a collection of data that exists and is organised around a specific theme or requirement. It can be of the 'flat-file' type, or it can have relational capabilities, as in the case of Access, which is known as a relational database management system (RDBMS).

The main difference between flat-file and relational database systems is that the latter can store and manipulate data in multiple 'tables', while the former systems can only manipulate a single table at any given time. To make accessing the data easier, each row (or **record**) of data within a database table is structured in the same fashion, i.e., each record will have the same number of columns (or **fields**).

We define a database and its various elements as:

Database   A collection of data organised for a specific theme in one or more tables.

Table   A two-dimensional structure in which data is stored, like in a spreadsheet

Record   A row of information in a table relating to a single entry and comprising one or more fields.

Field   A single column of information of the same type, such as people's names.

In Access 95 the maximum size of a database is 1 gigabyte and can include linked tables in other files. The number of objects in a database is limited to 32,768, while the maximum number of fields in a table is limited to 255.

A good example of a flat-file database is the invoicing details kept on clients by a company. These details could include name of client, description of work done, invoice number, and amount charged, as follows:

NAME	Consultancy	Invoice	Value
VORTEX Co. Ltd	Wind Tunnel Tests	9601	120.84
AVON Construction	Adhesive Tests	9602	103.52
BARROWS Associates	Tunnel Design Tests	9603	99.32
STONEAGE Ltd	Carbon Dating Tests	9604	55.98
PARKWAY Gravel	Material Size Tests	9605	180.22
WESTWOOD Ltd	Load Bearing Tests	9606	68.52

Such a flat-file DBMS is too limited for the type of information normally held by most companies. If the same client asks for work to be carried out regularly, then the details for that client (which could include address, telephone and fax numbers, contact name, date of invoice, etc., will have to be entered several times. This can lead to errors, but above all to redundant information being kept on a client - each entry will have to have the name of the client, their address, telephone and fax numbers.

The relational facilities offered by Access, overcome the problems of entry errors and duplication of information. The ability to handle multiple tables at any one time allows for the grouping of data into sensible subsets. For example, one table, called client, could hold the name of the client, their address, telephone and fax numbers, while another table, called invoice, could hold information on the work done, invoice number, date of issue, and amount charged. The two tables must have one unique common field, such as client reference number. The advantage is that details of each client are entered and stored only once, thus reducing the time and effort wasted on entering duplicate information, and also reducing the space required for data storage.

Hardware and Software Requirements

If Microsoft Access is already installed on your computer, you can safely skip the rest of this chapter.

To install and use Access for Windows 95, you need the following hardware and software configuration:

- An IBM-compatible computer equipped with Intel's 80386 (or higher) processor with a minimum processor speed of 33 megahertz (MHz).

- A hard disc with 49MB of free space for a full installation. You can save on hard disc space by electing to install only the components you require.

- A random access memory (RAM) of at least 12 megabytes (MB), as this is the memory size required to run the program efficiently. To manipulate large databases at a reasonable speed, this amount of RAM, and/or the speed of your processor will need to be increased.

- An operating system such as Windows 95, or Windows NT.

Realistically, to run a reasonably sized Microsoft Access database with relational capabilities, you will need a 486 or a Pentium PC, with 16MB of RAM. If you intend to use a database with linked or embedded pictures, then you will also need a SVGA display capability.

Although it is possible to operate Microsoft Access from the keyboard, the availability of a mouse is highly desirable. After all, pointing and clicking at an option on the screen to start an operation or command, is a lot easier than having to learn several different key combinations.

Installing Access

Installing Access on your computer's hard disc is made very easy with the use of the SETUP program, which even configures Access automatically to take advantage of the computer's hardware.

If you are installing from floppy discs, insert the first Setup disc (Disc 1) in the A: drive, or if you are installing from a CD-ROM, insert the CD in the CD-ROM drive. If you are installing from a network drive, make a note of the drive letter because you will need it later. Then do the following:

- Click the **Start** button on the Windows 95 Taskbar and select **S**ettings, **C**ontrol Panel.

- On the displayed Control Panel window, double-click the Add/Remove Programs icon, shown here.

- On the Add/Remove Programs Properties dialogue box, click the Install/Uninstall tab and press the **I**nstall button.

- SETUP will scan your disc for already installed parts of Microsoft Office and will advise you as to the folder in which you should install Access. This will most likely be **Msoffice** - we suggest you accept all the default options.

- Follow the SETUP instructions, and when the Microsoft Access for Windows 95 - Maintenance dialogue box appears on the screen, shown on the next page, press the **S**elect All button.

- If you are not likely to work on the same database on two different computers (at home and at work), then you could deselect the Microsoft Briefcase Replication option before going on.

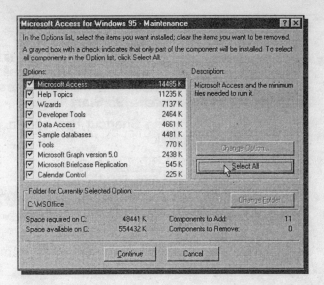

- Pressing **Continue** starts the installation of Microsoft Access.

- When a new disc is required (if you are installing from floppy discs), the installation program will inform you by displaying a similar dialogue box to the one shown here.

When all discs have been read, the SETUP program will modify your system files automatically so that you can start Access easily. It even detects your computer's processor and display, and configures Access to run smoothly with your system.

Finally, Access creates and displays a new entry in the **Start, Programs** cascade menu, with the icon shown here. Clicking this menu entry will start Microsoft Access. If you have MS-Office installed, SETUP also adds Access to the Microsoft Shortcut Bar facility (see overleaf).

The Office Shortcut Bar

The Microsoft Office Shortcut Bar, provides a convenient way to work with your documents and the Office applications (including Microsoft Access) by complementing the Windows 95 **Start** menu.

The various icons on the Shortcut Bar, shown below, have the following function:

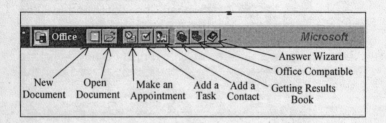

The Start a New Document button: Allows you to select in the displayed dialogue box the tab containing the type of document you want to work with. Double-clicking the type of document or template you want, automatically loads the appropriate application.

The Open a Document button: Allows you to work with an existing document. Opening a document, first starts the application originally used to create it.

The Schedule buttons: Allow you to schedule an appointment, schedule a task, and add a contact name.

Getting Results Book button: Provides you with suggestions on how to work efficiently with the Microsoft Office applications.

Office Compatible button: Provides demonstrations on applications which are compatible with Microsoft Office.

Answer Wizard button: Provides help on various topics which you might need while working with Office.

2. STARTING ACCESS

Access is started in Windows 95 either by clicking the **Start** button then selecting **Programs** and clicking on the 'Microsoft Access' icon on the cascade menu, or by clicking the 'Open a Document' icon on the Office Shortcut Bar and double-clicking on an Access database file. In the latter case the database will be loaded into Access at the same time.

When you start the Access program by double-clicking its icon, the following dialogue box is displayed on your screen:

From this dialogue box, you can either create a new database, or **Open an Existing Database**. If you select to create a new database, then you can elect either to create a **Blank Database**, or use the **Database Wizard** to help you with the creation of the new database.

Access for Windows 95 makes extensive use of Wizards, which have been designed to help the new user to create databases more easily. In particular, the Database Wizard builds the necessary elements for 22 different databases for both home and business use. All you have to do is to answer a set of questions and the Wizard builds the database.

Parts of the Access Screen

Before we start designing a database, let us take a look at the Access opening screen. Below we also show the *what's new* help topic displaying its list.

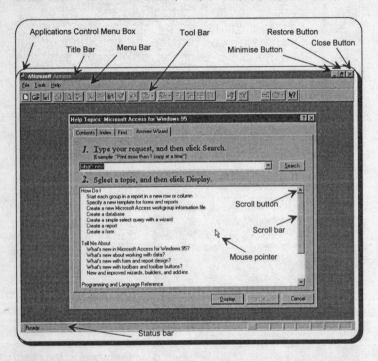

As you can see, these windows have some common screen elements with those of other MS Office applications.

Although more than one window can be displayed simultaneously, only one is the active window (which normally displays on top of any other non-active windows. Title bars of non-active windows appear a lighter shade than those of the active ones. In the above example, the Help Topics window is the active one. To activate the other window, click with the left mouse button anywhere within it.

The various screen areas have the following functions.

Area	Function
Command button	 Clicking on the command button, (see upper-left corner of the Access window), displays a pull-down menu which can be used to control the program window. It includes commands for restoring, moving, sizing, maximising, minimising, and closing the window.
Title bar	The bar at the top of a window which displays the application name and the name of the current document.
Minimise box	When clocked on, this button minimises the application to the Windows Taskbar.
Restore button	 When clicked on, this button restores the active window to the position and size that was occupied before it was maximised. The Restore button is then replaced by a Maximise button, as shown here, which is used to set the window to full screen size. 
Close button	 The extreme top right button that you click to close a window.

Menu bar	The bar below the Title bar which allows you to choose from several menu options. Clicking on a menu item displays the pull-down menu associated with that item. The options listed in the Menu bar depend on what you are doing at the time.
Toolbar	The bar below the Menu bar which contains buttons that give you mouse click access to the functions most often used in the program. These are grouped according to function.
Scroll Buttons	The arrowheads at each end of each scroll bar which you click to scroll the screen up and down one line, or left and right 10% of the screen, at a time.
Scroll Bars	The areas on the screen (extreme right and bottom of each window) that contain scroll boxes in vertical and horizontal bars. Clicking on these bars allows you to control the part of the window that might not be visible on the screen.
Status Bar	The bottom line of the window that displays status information, and in which a short help description appears when you point and click on a button.

The Menu Bar Options

Each window's menu bar option has associated with it a pull-down sub-menu. To activate the menu of a window, either press the <Alt> key, which causes the first option of the menu (in this case **File**) to be highlighted, then use the right and left arrow keys to highlight any of the options in the menu, or use the mouse to point to an option. Pressing either the <Enter> key, or the left mouse button, reveals the pull-down sub-menu of the highlighted menu option.

The sub-menu of the **File** option of the Access window, is shown below.

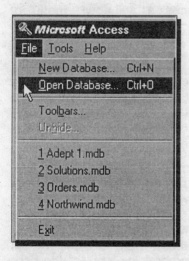

Menu options can also be activated directly by pressing the <Alt> key followed by the underlined letter of the required option. Thus pressing **Alt+F**, causes the pull-down sub-menu of **File** to be displayed. You can use the up and down arrow keys to move the highlighted bar up and down a sub-menu, or the right and left arrow keys to move along the options in the menu bar. Pressing the <Enter> key selects the highlighted option or executes the highlighted command. Pressing the <Esc> key once, closes the pull-down sub-menu, while pressing the <Esc> key for a second time, closes the menu system.

Furthermore, depending on what you are doing with Access, the items on the menu bar can be different from those of the opening screen.

For example, once a database is opened the menu bar changes to the following:

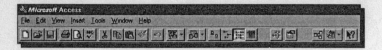

This is to be expected since available menu options reflect the type of work you are doing at the time. Similarly, the sub-menu under the **File** option of the above screen is different from the one of the Access opening screen. In general, menu options offer the following:

File

Produces a pull-down menu of mainly file related tasks, which allow you, amongst other things, to create a 'new' database, 'open' an existing database, 'rename' a database, 'print' a database, 'close' a database, and 'exit' the program.

Edit

Gives access to the most common editing tasks which can be applied on selected items. The pull-down menu has options which allow you to 'undo' changes made, 'cut', 'copy' and 'paste' text, and rename database components, such as tables, queries, forms, etc.

View

Gives you complete control on what you see on your screen. For example, you choose to view several database elements, such as tables, queries, forms, and reports, and view files as icons or lists. You can further select which toolbars you want to be displayed on the screen.

Insert	Allows you to insert tables, queries, forms, reports, macros, or modules. You can even use the AutoForm and AutoReport to create forms and reports automatically.
Tools	Allows you to spell-check your work, switch on the AutoCorrect facility, or use Office links. You can also add or change relationships between database tables, and allows you to specify the level of security required.
Window	Allows you to display multiple windows on the screen in 'cascade' or 'tile' form, or arrange icons within an active window.
Help	Allows you to choose how to get help, either by using the Microsoft Access Help Topics option, or by using the Answer Wizard (these will be discussed in some detail shortly). You can also open a window that displays basic details of the system and the available resources.

Some dialogue boxes display a '?' button on the right end of their title bar, as shown here. Clicking this button changes the mouse pointer from its usual inclined arrow shape to the 'What's this?' shape. Pointing to an object in the window and clicking, opens a Help topic.

For a more detailed description of each sub-menu item, either highlight it and read the text on the status bar, or use the on-line **Help** system.

The Mouse Pointers

In Access, as with all other graphical based programs, the use of a mouse makes many operations both easier and more fun to carry out.

Access makes use of the mouse pointers available in Windows 95, some of the most common of which are illustrated below. When the program is initially started up the first you will see is the hourglass, which turns into an upward pointing hollow arrow once the Access screen appears on your display. Other shapes depend on the type of work you are doing at the time.

The hourglass which displays when you are waiting while performing a function.

The arrow which appears when the pointer is placed over menus, scrolling bars, and buttons.

The I-beam which appears in normal text areas of the screen.

The large 4-headed arrow which appears after choosing the **Control, Move/Size** command(s) for moving or sizing windows.

The double arrows which appear when over the border of a window, used to drag the side and alter the size of the window.

The Help hand which appears in the Help windows, and is used to access 'hypertext' type links.

Microsoft Access, like other Windows packages, has additional mouse pointers which facilitate the execution of selected commands. Some of these are:

↓   The vertical pointer which appears when pointing over a column in a database table and used to select the column.

→   The horizontal pointer which appears when pointing at a row in a database table, and used to select the row.

    The slanted arrow which appears when the pointer is placed in the selection bar area of the Field Properties box of a database table.

◄‖►   The vertical split arrow which appears when pointing over the area separating two columns and used to size a column.

⬍   The horizontal split arrow which appears when pointing over the area separating two rows and used to size a row.

+   The frame cross which you drag to create a frame while designing a Form.

The shape of additional mouse pointers is self-evident.

Shortcut Menus

To see a shortcut menu containing the most common commands applicable to an item, point with your mouse at the item and click the right mouse button. For example, left-clicking the adjacent Open Database icon, displays the Open dialogue box. Right-clicking within the file list area of this dialogue box, displays the short-cut menu shown below, with the following options:

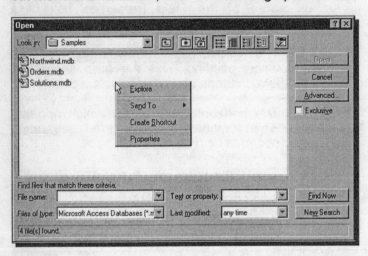

In the above case we have the option to **Explore** the contents of the logged folder (Samples), **Send To** the 3½" Floppy or the Briefcase its contents, **Create Shortcut** icons, or see the folder's **Properties**.

Right-clicking the **File name** box at the bottom of the dialogue box, displays a shortcut menu that gives you access to several editing commands. The commands, however, are only available to you if you have started typing a filename.

Having activated a shortcut menu, you can close it without taking any further action by simply pressing the <Esc> key.

Using Help in Access

The Microsoft Access Help Program provides on-line help in exactly the same way as the Help programs of the other MS-Office applications. You can use the **Help, Microsoft Access Help Topics** command, then click the Contents tab, to obtain the following:

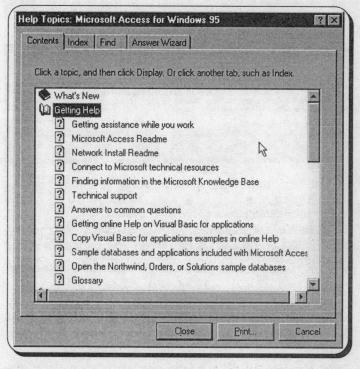

Help topics can be printed on paper by selecting the topic, then clicking the **Print** button.

Another way of obtaining help on a specific topic is to select the Answer Wizard, either by clicking its tab on the above window, or selecting it from the **Help** menu. You can then type your request in the top box and click the **Search** button, which lists the available information in the second box, as shown overleaf.

17

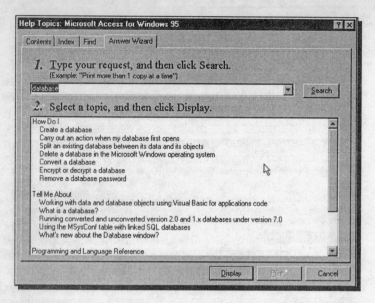

In addition, there are several ways to obtain on-line Help. These are:

On-line Help Messages: Access displays a command description in the Status bar when you choose a menu or command.

Context Sensitive Help: To get context sensitive help, click the Help button on the Toolbar, shown here, then move the modified mouse pointer to an area on the presentation or on to a particular Toolbar button and press the left mouse button.

3. DATABASE BASICS

Database Elements

Before we start designing a database using Microsoft Access, it will be a good idea if we looked at the various elements that make up a database. To do so, start Access, which opens the simple, three-menu option Access screen with the **File**, **Tools** and **Help** options on the Menu bar.

Next, and if this is being done immediately after starting Access, select the **Database Wizard** option on

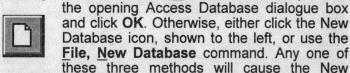

the opening Access Database dialogue box and click **OK**. Otherwise, either click the New Database icon, shown to the left, or use the **File, New Database** command. Any one of these three methods will cause the New Database dialogue box to be displayed, as follows:

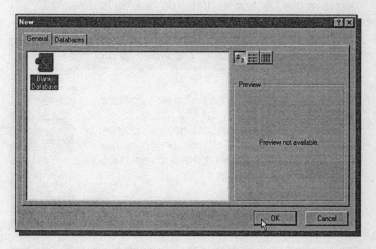

To create a new database, press the **OK** button. This opens the File New Database dialogue box shown on the next page.

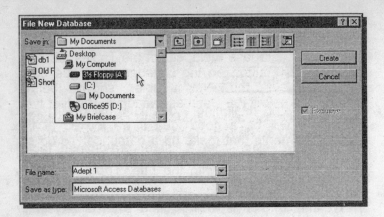

In the **File name** box, type the database name, say **ADEPT 1**, which replaces the default name **db1**. Access adds the extension **.MDB** which, however, you don't normally see. We also decided to save this example on floppy disc, therefore we clicked the down arrow against the **Save in** box and selected the **3½" Floppy (A:)** drive. Finally, pressing the **Create** button displays the Database dialogue box as follows:

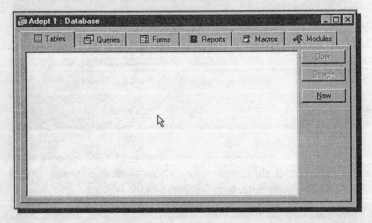

It is from here that you can design the various elements that make up a database, such as Tables, Queries, Forms, and Reports, all of which we will examine in some detail in the rest of the book.

Designing a Database Table

To design a database table, select the Tables tab and click the **New** button on the Database dialogue box, which displays the New Table, shown below immediately below the Database window. The first two options on the list, allow you to start designing a table from scratch, while the third option allows you to automatically select from a list of pre-defined table applications. The penultimate option allows you to import tables and objects from an external file into the current database, while the last option allows you to link a table in the current database to external tables.

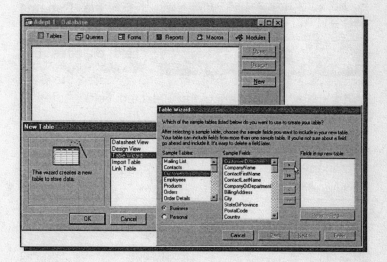

Selecting the third option and pressing **OK**, opens the Table Wizard dialogue box, shown at the lower right corner of the composite screen dump above.

The database we are going to create holds the invoicing details which the firm Adept Consultants keep on their clients. One table will hold the details of the clients, while another will hold the actual invoice details.

Choose 'Customers' from the **Sample Tables** list of the Table Wizard dialogue box, to reveal a list of appropriate fields for that table.

You can either select all the fields or you can select a few. For our example, we selected the following fields: CustomerID, CompanyName, BillingAddress, City, StateOrProvince, PostalCode, ContactTitle, PhoneNumber, FaxNumber and Notes, by highlighting each in turn and pressing the 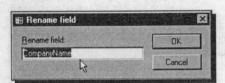 button.

Don't worry if these field names are not exactly what you want, as they can be easily changed. To change field names, highlight them in turn in the 'Fields in my new table' list and click the **Rename Field** button to reveal the Rename field dialogue box shown here.

We suggest you change the selected field names to those listed below.

CustomerID	CustomerID
CompanyName	Name
BillingAddress	Address
City	Town
StateOrProvince	County
PostalCode	PostCode
ContactTitle	Contact
PhoneNumber	Phone
FaxNumber	Fax
Notes	Order

When you have completed renaming the field names, press the **Finish** button, which displays the Customers Table ready for you to enter information.

Redesigning a Database Table:

To redesign the table, including changing its field

names, click the Design View icon shown here, or use the **View, Table Design** command. The following Table is displayed.

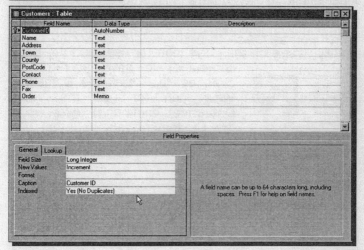

As each field name is highlighted, a Field Properties box appears at the bottom of the screen. If you were using this Table View to rename fields, then you should also edit the name appearing against the Caption property, or remove it altogether.

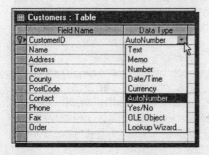

Next, place the cursor at the end of the Data Type descriptor of the CustomerID field which causes a down-arrow button to be displayed. Clicking this button, displays a drop-down list of data types, as shown here.

As we intend to use the first four letters of a company's name as the CustomerID field, change the current data type from Counter to Text. Similarly, change the data type of the last field (Order) from Memo to AutoNumber. Finally, place the cursor against the Phone and Fax fields and delete the entry against the Input Mask in the Field Properties box. The type of input mask displayed here is ideal for USA Phone and Fax numbers, but it does not correspond to the entry form usually adopted in the UK, so it is best removed.

Finally, first click the Save icon (or use the **File, Save**

command) to save your design changes, then click the Datasheet View icon (or use the **View, Datasheet** command) to revert to the Customers table so that you can start entering information, as shown below.

Customer ID	Name	Address	Town	County	Post Code	Contact
VORT	VORTEX Co. Ltd	Windy House	St. Austell	Cornwall	TR18 1FX	Brian Storm
AVON	AVON Construction	Riverside House	Stratford-on-Avon	Warwickshire	AV15 2QW	John Waters
BARR	BARROWS Associates	Barrows House	Bodmin	Cornwall	PL22 1XE	Mandy Brown
STON	STONEAGE Ltd	Data House	Salisbury	Wiltshire	SB44 1BN	Mike Irons
PARK	PARKWAY Gravel	Aggregate House	Bristol	Avon	BS55 2ZX	James Stone
WEST	WESTWOOD Ltd	Weight House	Plymouth	Devon	PL22 1AA	Mary Slim
GLOW	GLOWORM Ltd	Light House	Brighton	Sussex	BR87 4DD	Peter Summers
SILV	SILVERSMITH Co	Radiation House	Exeter	Devon	EX28 1PL	Adam Smith
WORM	WORMGLAZE Ltd	Glass House	Winchester	Hampshire	WN23 5TR	Richard Glazer
EALI	EALING Engines Design	Engine House	Taunton	Somerset	TN17 3RT	Trevor Miles
HIRE	HIRE Service Equipment	Network House	Bath	Avon	BA76 3WE	Nicole Webb
EURO	EUROBASE Co. Ltd	Control House	Penzance	Cornwall	TR15 8LK	Sarah Star

The widths of the above fields were changed so that all fields could be visible on the screen at the same time.

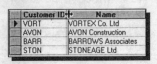

To change the width of a field, place the cursor on the column separator until the cursor changes to the vertical split arrow, then drag the column separator to the right or left, to increase or decrease the width of the field.

Sorting a Database Table

As you enter information into a database table, you might elect to change the field headings by clicking the Design Table icon and editing a field name, say from Name to CompanyName. If you do this, on return to the Customers table you will find that the records have sorted automatically in ascending order of the entries of the field in which you left the cursor while in the Design Table.

Contact	Phone	Fax	Order
Brian Storm	01776-223344	01776-224466	1
John Waters	01657-113355	01657-221133	2
Mandy Brown	01554-664422	01554-663311	3
Mike Irons	01765-234567	01765-232332	4
James Stone	01534-987654	01534-984567	5
Mary Slim	01234-667755	01234-669988	6
Peter Summers	01432-746523	01432-742266	7
Adam Smith	01336-997755	01336-996644	8
Richard Glazer	01123-654321	01123-651234	9
Trevor Miles	01336-010107	01336-010109	10
Nicole Webb	01875-558822	01875-552288	11
Sarah Star	01736-098765	01736-098567	12
			(AutoNumber)

If you want to preserve the order in which you entered your data, then sort by the last field (Order) with its type as AutoNumber. This can be done at any time, even after you finished entering all other information in your table.

Sorting a database table in ascending order of an AutoNumber type field, results in the database table displaying in the order in which the data was originally entered in that table. Above, we show the Contact field, so that you can cross-check the original order of your Customer table, as well as the rest of the information in that table not shown in the screen dump of the previous page.

To sort a database table in ascending or descending order of the entries of any field, place the cursor in the required field and click the Sort Ascending or Sort Descending icon, shown here.

With the keyboard, select the **Records, Sort** command, then choose either the **Ascending** or the **Descending** option.

Applying a Filter to a Sort:

If you would like to sort and display only records that fit selected criteria, use the **Records, Filter, Advanced Filter/Sort** command, which opens the Filter dialogue box, shown below.

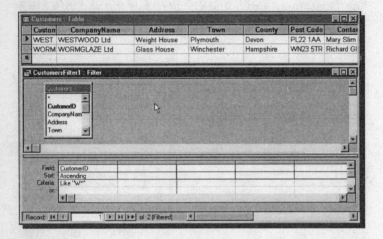

The upper portion of the dialogue box displays all the fields in the Customers table, while the lower portion is where you enter your filter restrictions. In the above example, we chose to view, in ascending order, the records within the CustomersID field that start with W - we typed W* and Access displayed *Like "W*"*.

On pressing the Apply Filter icon, the Customers table displays with only two entries, as seen in the above composite screen dump. To revert to the display of all the records, click the same icon again, which now appears on the Toolbar depressed, and bears the name Remove Filter.

Using a Database Form

Once a table has been selected from the Database window, clicking the down-arrow against the New Object button and selecting AutoForm, automatically displays each record of that table in form view. The created form for the Customers table is shown below.

Forms can be used to enter, change or view data. They are mainly used to improve the way in which data is displayed on the screen.

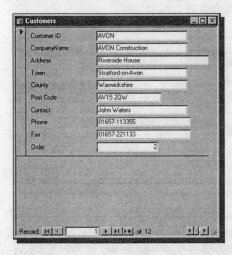

Forms can also be used to sort records in a database table in ascending or descending order of a selected field.

When you attempt to close a new Form window, you will be asked whether you would like to save it. An Access database can have lots of different forms, each designed with a different purpose in mind. Saved forms are displayed in the Database window when you press the Form button. In the above example, we chose the default name suggested by Access, which was Customers.

In a later chapter we will discuss Form design in some detail, including their customisation.

Working with Data

Adding Records in a Table: Whether you are in Table view or Form view, to add a record, click the New icon, shown here.

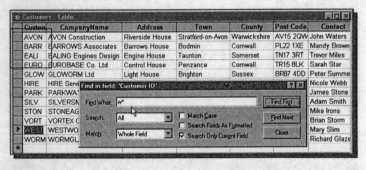

When in Table view, the cursor jumps to the first empty record in the table (the one with the asterisk in the box to the left of the first field). When in Form view, Access displays an empty form which can be used to add a new record.

Finding Records in a Table: Whether you are in Table or Form view, to find a record click the Find icon, or use **Edit, Find**. This opens the following dialogue box:

Note the field name on the Title bar, which is CustomerID, indicating that the cursor was in the CustomerID field before we clicked the Find icon or selected the **Find** command.

To find all the records starting with **w**, we type **w*** in the **Fi_nd What** box of the dialogue box. If the **Search Only Current Field** box is ticked, the search is carried out in that field. Pressing the **Find First** button, highlights the first record with the CustomerID 'WEST'. Pressing the **Find Next** button, highlights the next record that matches our selected criteria.

Deleting Records from a Table: To delete a record when in Table view, point to the box to the left of the record to highlight the entire record, as shown below, then press the <Del> key.

	WEST	WESTWOOD Ltd	Weight House	Plymouth	Devon	PL22 1AA
▶	WORM	WORMGLAZE Ltd	Glass House	Winchester	Hampshire	WN23 5TR
✳						

To delete a record when in Form view, first display the record you want to delete, then use the **Edit, Select Record** command to select the whole record, and press the <Del> key.

In both cases you will be given a warning and you will be asked to confirm your decision.

Delete, Insert, and Move Fields in a Table: To delete a field from a table, close any forms that might be open, then load the table from the Database window, then press the Design View icon, click the row selector to highlight the field you want to remove, as shown below, and press the Delete Row icon, shown here, or use the **Edit, Delete Row** command.

⊞ Customers : Table		
Field Name	Data Type	
🔑 CustomerID	Text	
CompanyName	Text	
▶ Address	Text	
Town	Text	
County	Text	
Post Code	Text	

To insert a field in a table, display the table in Design View, and highlight the field above which you want to insert the new field, and press the Insert Row icon, shown here, or use the **Insert, Field** command.

To move a field from its current to a new position in a table, select the field you want to move, then point to the row selector so that the mouse pointer is inclined as shown below, and drag the row to its new position.

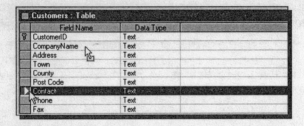

Note that while you are dragging the field, the mouse pointer changes to the one pointing at the Name field in the above composite. Releasing the mouse button, moves the Contact field to where the CompanyName field is now and pushes all other fields one row down.

Printing a Table View:

You can print a database table by clicking the Print

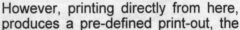

icon, or you can preview it on screen by clicking the Preview icon.

However, printing directly from here, produces a pre-defined print-out, the

format of which you cannot control effectively. Although you can control the margins and print orientation by pressing the **Setup** or **Properties** button, you cannot control the printed font size.

For a better method of producing a printed output, see the Report Design section.

4. RELATIONAL DATABASE DESIGN

In order to be able to discuss relational databases, we will add to the database of the previous chapter an Orders table. To do this go through the following steps.

- Open the **ADEPT 1** database and use the **New** button on the Database window to add an Orders table to it.

- Use the Table Wizard and select Orders from the displayed **Sample Tables** list. Next, select the five fields displayed below under **Fields in my new table** from the **Sample Fields** list, and press the **Next** button.

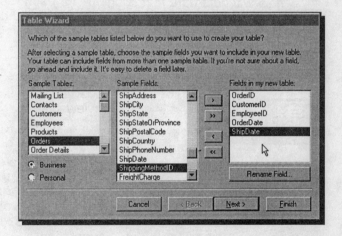

This displays the top dialogue box on the next page, in which you can, if you want to, change the name of the table. We selected to accept the default name, but we clicked the 'No, I'll set the primary key' radio button before pressing the **Next** key.

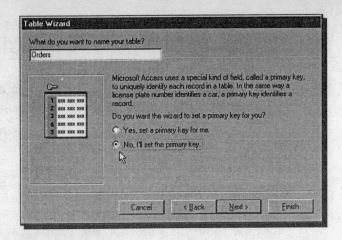

On the next dialogue box you can select which field will hold data that is unique for each record. The key field must be unique in a table, and the OrderID field satisfies this requirement. This field is used by Access for fast searches.

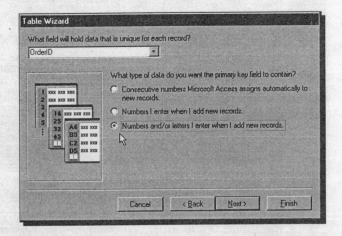

Click the **Numbers and/or letters I enter when I add new records** radio button, before you press the **Next** button.

On the next dialogue box you specify whether the new table is related to any other tables in the database. The default is that it is not related.

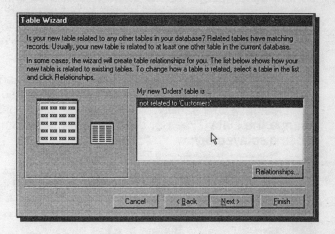

Accept the default option, and press the **Next** button to reveal the final dialogue box.

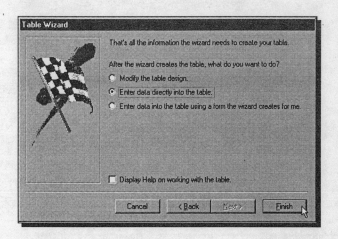

Select the second option and press the **Finish** button, to let the Wizard create your table.

Although the two tables are actually related, we chose at this stage to tell the Wizard that they are not. This might appear to you as odd, but the Wizard makes certain assumptions about unique fields (for example, that ID fields are numbers), which is not what we want them to be. We choose to remain in control of the design of our database and, therefore, we will define the relationship between the two tables later.

The Wizard displays the newly created table ready for you to enter your data. However, before doing so, use the Design Table facility, as discussed previously, to change the Data Types of the selected Field Names to those displayed below.

	Field Name	Data Type	
🔑	OrderID	Text	
	CustomerID	Text	
▶	EmployeeID	Text	▼
	OrderDate	Date/Time	
	ShipDate	Date/Time	

Orders : Table

The information you need to enter in the Orders table is shown below.

Orders : Table

Order ID	Customer ID	Employee ID	Order Date	Ship Date
94085VOR	VORT	A.D. Smith	20/03/95	10/04/95
94097AVO	AVON	W.A. Brown	25/03/95	14/04/95
94099BAR	BARR	S.F. Adams	01/04/95	02/05/95
95002STO	STON	C.H. Wills	20/04/95	25/05/95
95006PAR	PARK	A.D. Smith	13/05/95	16/06/95
95010WES	WEST	W.A. Brown	15/05/95	26/06/95
95018GLO	GLOW	L.S. Stevens	25/06/95	19/07/95
95025SIL	SILV	S.F. Adams	28/06/95	22/07/95
95029WOR	WORM	C.H. Wills	20/07/95	13/08/95
95039EAL	EALI	A.D. Smith	30/07/95	25/08/95
95045HIR	HIRE	W.A. Brown	18/08/95	08/09/95
95051EUR	EURO	L.S. Stevens	25/08/95	19/09/95
▶ 95064AVO	AVON	S.F. Adams	20/09/95	15/10/95

Record: 13 of 13

Relationships

Information held in two or more tables of a database is normally related in some way. In our case, the two tables, Customers and Orders, are related by the CustomerID field.

To build up relationships between tables, return to the Database window and press the Relationships icon on the Tool bar, shown here. This opens the following window in which the index field in each table is emboldened.

You can build relationships between tables by dragging a field name from one table into another. In our example below, we have dragged CustomerID from the Customers table (by pointing to it, pressing the left

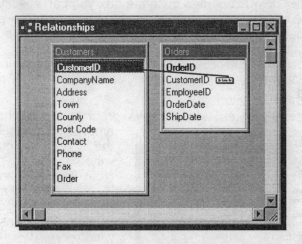

mouse button, and while keeping the mouse button pressed, dragging the pointer) to the required field in the other table, in this case CustomerID in the Orders table. Releasing the mouse button opens the dialogue boxes shown at the top of the next page (the second one by pressing the **Join Type** button on the first one).

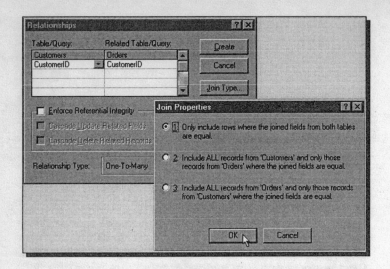

In the Join Properties dialogue box you can specify the type of join Access should create in new queries - more about this later. For the present, press the **OK** button on the Join Properties dialogue box, to close it, then check the **Enforce Referential Integrity** box in the Relationships dialogue box, and press the **Create** button.

Access creates and displays graphically the chosen

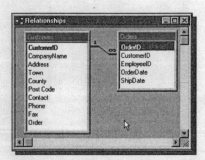

type of relationship in the Relationships window shown here. Note the relationship '1 customer to many (∞) orders' symbolism in the Relationships window.

Because Access is a relational database, data can be used in queries from more than one table at a time. As we have seen, if the database contains tables with related data, the relationships can be defined easily.

Usually, the matching fields have the same name, as in our example of Customers and Orders tables. In the Customers table, the CustomersID field is the primary field and relates to the CustomersID field in the Orders table - there can be several orders in the Orders table from one customer in the Customers table.

The various types of relationships are as follows:

- Inherited - for attaching tables from another Access database. The original relationships of the attached database can be used in the current database.

- Referential - for enforcing relationships between records according to certain rules, when you add or delete records in related tables belonging to the same database. For example, you can only add records to a related table, if a matching record already exists in the primary table, and you cannot delete a record from the primary table if matching records exist in a related table.

Viewing and Editing Relationships:

To view the current relationships between tables, activate the Database window and press the Relationships icon. This displays the following:

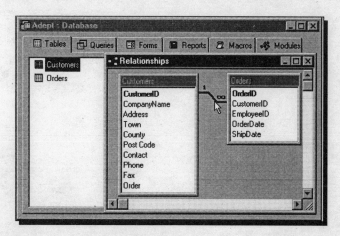

To edit a relationship, double-click the left mouse button at the pointer position shown on the previous screen dump. The tip of the mouse pointer must be on the inclined line joining the two tables in the Relationships window, as shown, before Access will respond. If you have difficulty with this action, first point to the relationship line and click once to embolden it, then use the **Relationships, Edit Relationship** command. Either of these two actions will open the Relationships dialogue box in which you can change the various options already discussed.

A given relationship can easily be removed altogether, by first activating it (pointing and clicking to embolden it), then pressing the <Del> key. A confirmation dialogue box will be displayed. To delete a table, you must first detach it from other tables, then select it in the Database Window and press the <Del> key. Think before you do this!

Creating an Additional Table

As an exercise, create a third table using the **Table Wizards** and select Invoices from the displayed **Sample Tables** list. Next, select the five fields displayed below - the names and their data types have been changed using the Design Table facility.

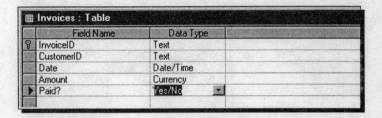

Field Name	Data Type	
InvoiceID	Text	
CustomerID	Text	
Date	Date/Time	
Amount	Currency	
Paid?	Yes/No	▼

Next, enter the data given below and build up appropriate relationships between the Invoices table, the Customers table and the Orders table, as shown on the next page.

Invoice No	Customer ID	Date	Amount	Paid?
AD9501	VORT	10/04/95	£120.84	☐
AD9502	AVON	14/04/95	£103.52	☑
AD9503	BARR	02/05/95	£99.32	☐
AD9504	STON	25/05/95	£55.98	☐
AD9505	PARK	16/06/95	£180.22	☐
AD9506	WEST	26/06/95	£68.52	☐
AD9507	GLOW	19/07/95	£111.56	☐
AD9508	SILV	22/07/95	£123.45	☑
AD9509	WORM	13/08/95	£35.87	☐
AD9510	EALI	25/08/95	£58.95	☐
AD9511	HIRE	08/09/95	£290.00	☐
AD9512	EURO	19/09/95	£150.00	☐
AD9513	AVON	15/10/95	£135.00	☐
				☐

The relationships between the three tables should be arranged as follows:

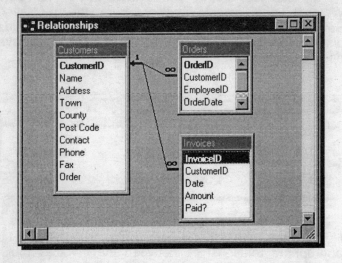

It is important that you should complete this exercise, as it consolidates what we have done so far and, in any case, we will be using all three tables in what comes next. So go ahead and try it.

5. CREATING A QUERY

You create a query so that you can ask questions about the data in your database tables. For example, we could find out whether we have more than one order from the same customer in our Adept database.

To do this, start Access, load **ADEPT 1**, and in the Database window click the Queries tab, followed by the **New** button which opens the New Query dialogue box. Selecting the **Find Duplicates Query Wizard**, displays the following:

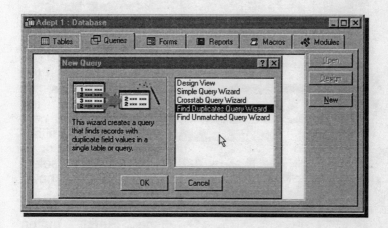

If, on clicking **OK**, Access tells you that this option is not available, then you must close down all running programs, then use the Access SETUP to add the Developer's Tools option to your installation. This can be done easily by placing the first Access distribution disc in the A: drive and using the Windows 95 **Start**, **Run** option, typing **a:\setup** in the displayed dialogue box, and checking the Developer's Tools option.

If the Developer's Tools option is already installed, then the Find Duplicates Query Wizard dialogue box is displayed, as shown on the next page.

From the displayed database tables in this dialogue box, select the Orders table and press the **Next** button.

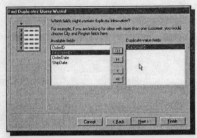

On the following dialogue box select **CustomerID** as the field you want to check for duplicate values, then press the ⟩ button, followed by the **Next** button.

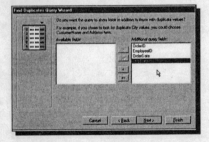

Finally, select the additional fields you would like to see along with the duplicate values, by selecting those you want from the next dialogue box, either one at a time or, if you decide to select all of them, as shown here, by clicking the ⟫ button. Clicking the **Finish** button displays the following Select Query screen.

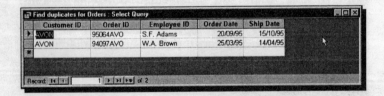

If you examine the original Orders table, you will indeed find that it contains two orders from AVON.

42

Types of Queries

The query we have created so far, is known as the *Select Query*, which is the most common type of query. However, with Access you can also create and use other types of queries, as follows:

- **Crosstab query** - used to present data with row and column headings, just like a spreadsheet. It can be used to summarise large amounts of data in a more readable form.

- **Action query** - used to make changes to many records in one operation. For example, you might like to remove from a given table all records that meet certain criteria, make a new table, or append records to a table. Obviously, this type of query has to be treated with care!

- **Union query** - used to match fields from two or more tables.

- **Pass-through query** - used to pass commands to an SQL (see below) database.

- **Data-definition query** - used to create, change, or delete tables in an Access database using SQL statements.

SQL stands for Structured Query Language, often used to query, update, and manage relational databases. Each query created by Access has an associated SQL statement that defines the action of that query. Thus, if you are familiar with SQL, you can use such statements to view and modify queries, or set form and report properties. However, these actions can be done more easily with the QBE (query-by-example) grid, to be discussed next. If you design union queries, pass-through queries, or data-definition queries, then you must use SQL statements, as these type of queries can not be designed with the QBE grid. Finally, to create a sub-query, you use the QBE grid, but you enter an SQL SELECT statement for criteria, as we shall see in the next QBE grid example.

The Query Window

The Query window is a graphical query-by-example (QBE) tool. Because of Access' graphical features, you can use the mouse to select, drag, and manipulate objects in the query window to define how you would like to see your data.

An example of a ready made Query window can be seen by selecting the Find duplicates for Orders query and clicking the **Design** button on the Database window. This action opens the Select Query dialogue box shown below.

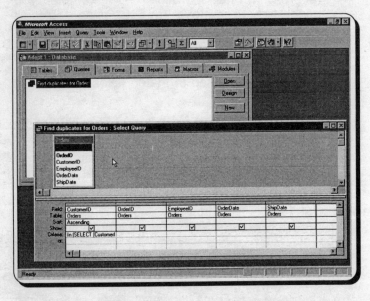

You can add a table to the top half of the Query window by simply dragging the table from the Database window. Similarly, you can add fields to the bottom half of the Query window (the QBE grid) by dragging fields from the tables on the top half of the Query window. In addition, the QBE grid is used to select the sort order of the data, or insert criteria, such as SQL statements.

To see the full SQL SELECT statement written by Access as the criteria selection when we first defined the query, widen the width of the first field, as follows:

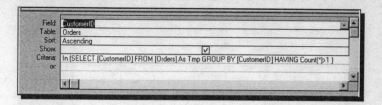

Note the part of the statement which states 'As Tmp GROUP'. Access collects the data you want as a temporary group, called a *dynaset*. This special set of data behaves like a table, but it is not a table; it is a dynamic view of the data from one or more tables, selected and sorted by the particular query.

Creating a New Query:

Below, we show a screen dump created by first clicking the Queries tab, then pressing the **New** button on the Database window. In the displayed New Query dialogue box, select Design View and press the **OK** button. This opens both the Select Query and the Show Table dialogue boxes shown overleaf.

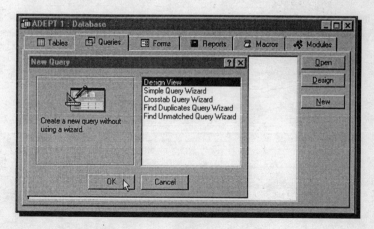

The Invoices and Customers tables were then added to the Select Query window, as shown below.

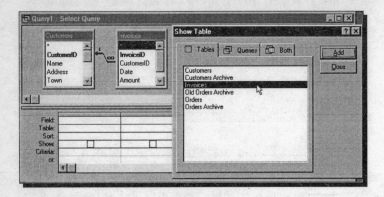

Adding Fields to a Query Window:

Below we show a screen in which the Paid? and InvoiceID fields have been dragged from the Invoices table and added to the Query window. In addition, the Name and Contact fields have been dragged from the Customers table and placed on the Query window, while the Phone field from the Customers table is about to be added to the Query window.

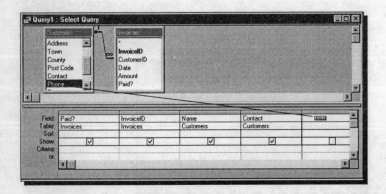

Having dragged all five fields from the two tables onto the QBE grid, we have added the word No as the criteria on the Paid? field and selected Ascending as the Sort for the InvoiceID field.

Note that the Invoices and Customers tables are joined by a line that connects the two CustomerID fields. The join line was created when we designed the tables and their relationships in the previous chapter. Even if you have not created these relationships, Access will join the tables in a query automatically when the tables are added to a query, provided each table has a field with the same name and a compatible data type and one of those fields is a primary key. A primary field is displayed in bold in the Query window.

If you have not created relationships between your tables yourself, or Access has not joined your tables automatically, you can still use related data in your query by joining the tables in the Query window.

Clicking the Run icon on the Toolbar, shown here, instantly displays all the unpaid invoices with the details you have asked for, as follows:

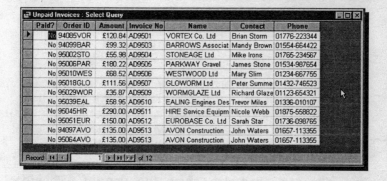

Paid?	Order ID	Amount	Invoice No	Name	Contact	Phone
No	94085VOR	£120.84	AD9501	VORTEX Co. Ltd	Brian Storm	01776-223344
No	94099BAR	£99.32	AD9503	BARROWS Associat	Mandy Brown	01554-664422
No	95002STO	£55.98	AD9504	STONEAGE Ltd	Mike Irons	01765-234567
No	95006PAR	£180.22	AD9505	PARKWAY Gravel	James Stone	01534-987654
No	95010WES	£68.52	AD9506	WESTWOOD Ltd	Mary Slim	01234-667755
No	95018GLO	£111.56	AD9507	GLOWORM Ltd	Peter Summe	01432-746523
No	95029WOR	£35.87	AD9509	WORMGLAZE Ltd	Richard Glaze	01123-654321
No	95039EAL	£58.95	AD9510	EALING Engines Des	Trevor Miles	01336-010107
No	95045HIR	£290.00	AD9511	HIRE Service Equipm	Nicole Webb	01875-558822
No	95051EUR	£150.00	AD9512	EUROBASE Co. Ltd	Sarah Star	01736-098765
No	94097AVO	£135.00	AD9513	AVON Construction	John Waters	01657-113355
No	95064AVO	£135.00	AD9513	AVON Construction	John Waters	01657-113355

Record: ◄ ◄ | 1 ► ►► ►* | of 12

To save your newly created query, use the **File, Save As/Export** command, and give it a name such as 'Unpaid Invoices' in the Save As dialogue box.

Types of Criteria

Access accepts the following expressions as criteria:

Arithmetic Operators		Comparison Operators		Logical Operators	
*	Multiply	<	Less than	And	And
/	Divide	<=	Less than or equal	Or	Inclusive or
+	Add	>	Greater than	Xor	Exclusive or
-	Subtract	>=	Greater than or equal	Not	Not equivalent
		=	Equal	Eqv	Equivalent
		<>	Not equal	Imp	Implication

Other operators		
Between	Between 50 And 150	All values between 50 and 150
In	In("Bath","Bristol")	All records with Bath and Bristol
Is	Is Null	All records with no value in that field
Like	Like "Brian *"	All records with Brian something in field
&	[Name]&" "&[Surname]	Concatenates strings

Using Wildcard Characters in Criteria:

In the previous example we used the criteria A* to mean any company whose name starts with the letter A. The asterisk in this criteria is known as a wildcard character.

To search for a pattern, you can use the asterisk (*) and the question mark (?) as wildcard characters when specifying criteria in expressions. An asterisk stands for any number of characters, while a question mark stands for any single character in the same position as the question mark.

The following examples show the use of wildcard characters in various types of expressions:

Entered Expression	Meaning	Examples
a?	Any two-letter word beginning with A	am, an, as, at
???d	Any four-letter word ending with d	find, hand, land, yard
Sm?th	Any five-letter word beginning with Sm and ending with th	Smith, Smyth
fie*	Any word starting with the letters fie	field, fiend, fierce, fiery
*ght	Any word ending with ght	alight, eight, fight, light, might, sight
*/5/95	All dates in May '95	1/5/95
a	Any word with the letter a in it	Brian, Mary, star, yard

Combining Criteria

By specifying additional criteria in a Query window you can create powerful queries for viewing your data. In the examples below we have added the field Amount to our Unpaid Invoices query.

The AND Criteria with Different Fields: When you insert criteria in several fields, but in the same row, Access assumes that you are searching for records that meet all of the criteria. For example, the criteria below list the records shown on the next page.

Field:	Paid?	Amount	InvoiceID	Name	Contact
Table:	Invoices	Invoices	Invoices	Customers	Customers
Sort:					
Show:	☑	☑	☑	☑	☑
Criteria:	No	Between 50 And 150			Like "M*"
or:					

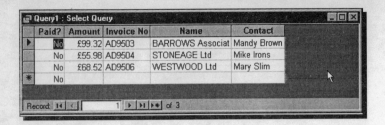

The OR Criteria with the Same Field: If you include multiple criteria in one field only, then Access assumes that you are searching for records that meet any one of the specified criteria. For example, the criteria <50 or >100 in the field Amount, shown below, list the required records, only if the No in the Paid? field is inserted in both rows.

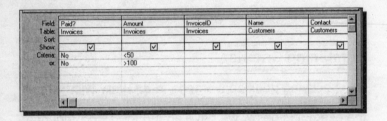

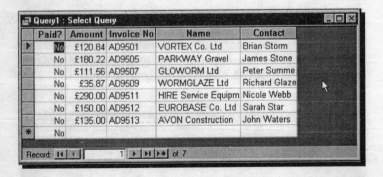

The OR Criteria with Different Fields: If you include multiple criteria in different fields, but in different rows, then Access assumes that you are searching for records that meet either one or the other of the specified criteria. For example, the criteria Yes in the Paid? field and the criteria <50 in the Amount field, but in different rows, list the following records.

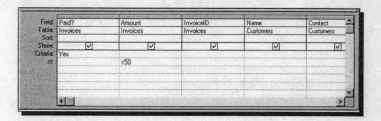

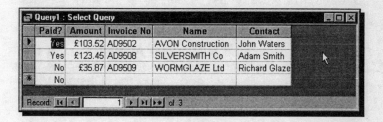

The AND and OR Criteria Together: The following choice of criteria will cause Access to retrieve either records that have Yes in the Paid? field and the company's name starts with the letter A, or records that the invoice amount is less than £50.

The retrieved records from such a query are shown below.

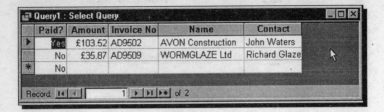

	Paid?	Amount	Invoice No	Name	Contact
▶	Yes	£103.52	AD9502	AVON Construction	John Waters
	No	£35.87	AD9509	WORMGLAZE Ltd	Richard Glaze
*	No				

Record: ◀◀ ◀ [1] ▶ ▶◀ ▶* of 2

Creating Calculated Fields

Let us assume that we would like to increase the amounts payable on all invoices overdue by more than 30 days from today by 0.5%, as a penalty for not settling an account on time. We can achieve this by creating a calculated field in our database.

To create a calculated field, open **ADEPT 1**, click the Query tab on the Database window, double-click the Unpaid Invoices query, and click the Design View button on the Toolbar. Next, insert a field after the Amount field using the **Insert Column** command, and type in the Field row of the newly inserted empty column, the following information:

```
New Amount:[Amount]*1.005
```

where *New Amount:* is our chosen name for the calculated field - the colon is essential. If you do not supply a name for the calculated field, Access uses the default name *Expr1:*, which you can rename later. The square brackets enclosing the word Amount in the above expression indicate a field name.

 Next, click the Properties button, shown here, or use the **View, Properties** command, to set the Format property to Currency.

52

Finally, add the Date field from the Invoices table to our query and type the expression <#01/05/95# in its Criteria field - the hash marks and leading zeros are supplied by Access if you do not type them yourself.

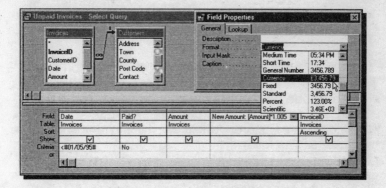

Clicking the Datasheet View button on the Toolbar, displays the following screen:

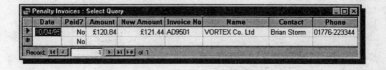

We suggest you save this query under the name Penalty Invoices.

Using Functions in Criteria

There are several functions that you can use in a calculated field of an Access query which can either be applied to extract information from a text field or date fields, or be used to calculate totals of entries.

Finding Part of a Text Field:

Let us assume that you want to find information that is part of a text field, like the area code (first 5 numbers) in the Phone field of our Customers table. To help you search a table for only part of a text field, Access provides three string functions. The syntax of these functions is as follows:

```
Left(stringexpr,n)
Right(stringexpr,n)
Mid(stringexpr,start,n)
```

The *stringexpr* argument can be either a field name or a text expression, while *n* is the number of characters you are searching for, and *start* is the position of the first character you want to start from.
Thus, to extract the area code of the text field Phone in our Customers table, we would type in the Field row of an empty field, either

```
Area Codes:Left([Phone],5)
```
or
```
Area Codes:Mid([Phone],1,5)
```

Note that to distinguish between the name of a field and a text expression, the name of the field is enclosed in square brackets.

The result of such a query is displayed on the next page.

Paid?	Order ID	Amount	Invoice No	Name	Contact	Phone	Area Codes
No	94085VOR	£120.84	AD9501	VORTEX Co. Ltd	Brian Storm	01776-223344	01776
No	94099BAR	£99.32	AD9503	BARROWS Associates	Mandy Brown	01554-664422	01554
No	95002STO	£55.98	AD9504	STONEAGE Ltd	Mike Irons	01765-234567	01765
No	95006PAR	£180.22	AD9505	PARKWAY Gravel	James Stone	01534-987654	01534
No	95010WES	£68.52	AD9506	WESTWOOD Ltd	Mary Slim	01234-667755	01234
No	95018GLO	£111.56	AD9507	GLOWORM Ltd	Peter Summers	01432-746523	01432
No	95029WOR	£35.87	AD9509	WORMGLAZE Ltd	Richard Glazer	01123-654321	01123
No	95039EAL	£58.95	AD9510	EALING Engines Design	Trevor Miles	01336-010107	01336
No	95045HIR	£290.00	AD9511	HIRE Service Equipment	Nicole Webb	01875-558822	01875
No	95051EUR	£150.00	AD9512	EUROBASE Co. Ltd	Sarah Star	01736-098765	01736
No	94097AVO	£135.00	AD9513	AVON Construction	John Waters	01657-113355	01657
No	95064AVO	£135.00	AD9513	AVON Construction	John Waters	01657-113355	01657

Record: 1 of 12

Finding Part of a Date Field:

To extract part of a date field, such as the month in which unpaid invoices were issued, type

```
Month:DatePart("m",[Date])
```

in the Field row of an empty field.

To extract the year in which unpaid invoices were issued, type

```
Year:DatePart("yyyy",[Date])
```

in the Field row of an empty field. This function returns the year in four digits, such as 1995.

Calculating Totals in Queries:

It is possible that you might want to know the total value of outstanding invoices grouped by month. Access allows you to perform calculations on groups of records using *totals* queries, also known as *aggregate* queries.

The table overleaf lists the functions that can be used

in queries to display totals. These functions are entered in the Totals row of a query which can be displayed by clicking the Totals button, shown here, while in Design View.

Function	Used to Find
Avg	The average of values in a field
Count	The number of values in a field
First	The field value from the first record in a table or query
Last	The field value from the last record in a table or query
Max	The highest value in a field
Min	The lowest value in a field
StDev	The standard deviation of values in a field
Sum	The total of values in a field
Var	The variance of values in a field

Below we show the one-table query to find the total of values of unpaid invoices grouped by month.

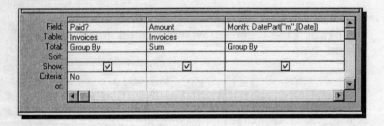

The retrieved records from such a query are shown below. We have named the query 'Monthly Invoices'.

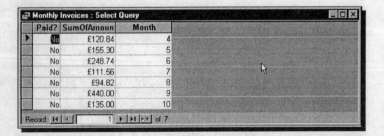

6. ADVANCED QUERIES

We have seen in the last chapter how to create a query with fields taken from two tables. The query in question was the Unpaid Invoices, shown below in Design View.

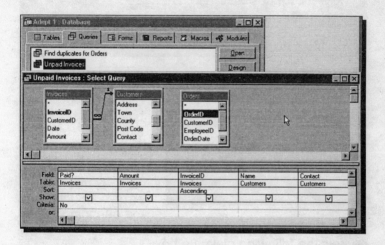

In order to make it easy for us to know which field in the above query comes from which table, Access displays the name of the table by default. This option is controlled from the **View, Table Names** command when in design View. When this menu option is ticked, Access adds the Table row in the QBE grid.

Now, suppose we would like to add the Orders table so that we can see the OrdersID field in extracted records of our query. To do this, click the Add Table button,

 shown here, which opens the Add Table dialogue box. Select Orders and click the **Add** button, then drag the OrdersID field onto the QBE grid, as shown overleaf.

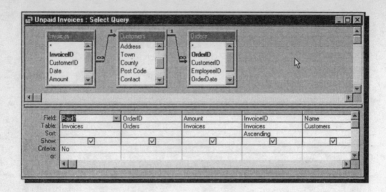

However, when you now click the Datasheet View button on the Tool bar to see the extracted records, Access displays the following message:

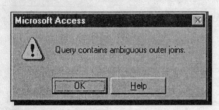

To correct this error, double-click the offending join to find out what type of join we have in this case, which reveals the following dialogue box:

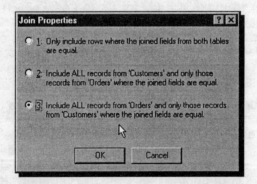

Obviously, option 3 is the wrong join. What we really need, is option 2. Select it to extract the correct records.

Types of Joins

Microsoft Access supports the following types of joins:

Types of joins	Effect
Equi-joins or Inner joins	A join in which records from two tables are combined and added to a dynaset only when there are equal values in the joined fields. For example, you can find records that show orders placed by each customer, with the dynaset containing only records for customers who have placed orders.
Outer joins	A join in which all the records from one table are added to the dynaset, and only those records from the other table for which values in the joined fields are equal. For example, you can find records that show all customers together with any orders they have placed.
Self-joins	A join in which records from one table are combined with other records from the same table when there are matching values in the joined fields. A self-join can be an equi-join or an outer join.

For an inner join, select option 1 from the Join Properties dialogue box. For an outer join, select option 2 or 3, depending on which records you want to include.

For example, choosing option 2 (also called a *left outer join*), in the case of our previous example, displays all the required records from the Customers table and only those records from Orders where the joined fields are equal. Option 3 (also called a *right outer join*), on the other hand, attempts to display all records in Orders and only those records from Customers where the joined fields are equal, resulting in some confusion in our particular example.

Creating a Parameter Query

A *Parameter Query* is a variation of the *Select Query* - the type we have been using so far. A Parameter Query is used when you frequently run the same query, but change the criteria each time you run it. Instead of having to make changes to the QBE grid, the design of a Parameter Query causes Access to prompt you for criteria. This type of query is particularly useful when used as a filter with forms.

To design a Parameter Query, design a **New** query in the normal way (do not use the Query Wizards), or change an existing Select Query. We have chosen the latter route and selected to change the Penalty Invoices query. In Design View, this now looks as follows:

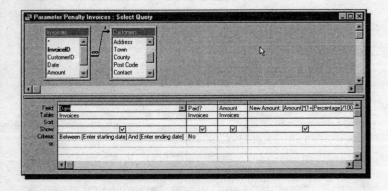

Note the two changes made to the above query. In the Date field we have entered two prompts (in square brackets) in the Criteria row, namely

```
[Enter starting date]
[Enter ending date]
```

and in the calculated field we have replaced the *1.005 by

```
*(1+[Percentage]/100)
```

60

Running this query, causes Access to ask for input values on three successive Enter Parameter Value boxes, as shown in the composite screen dump below:

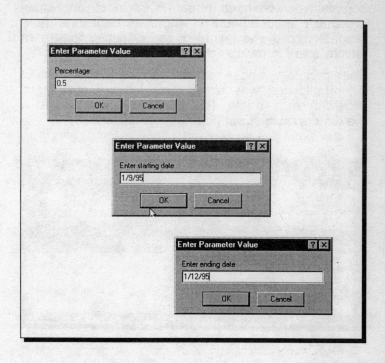

Providing the appropriate input information, displays the result of the search, as follows:

We have saved this query under the name Parameter Penalty Invoices.

Creating a Crosstab Query

You create a *Crosstab Query* to display totals in a compact, spreadsheet format. A Crosstab query can present a large amount of summary data in a more readable form. The layout of the extracted data from such a query is ideal as the basis for a report.

For example, suppose we wanted to examine which of our employees was responsible for our customers' orders in each month. The information is contained in the Orders table of our database as follows:

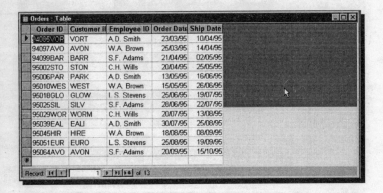

From the way this information is presented it is very difficult to work out who was responsible for which order in a given month. However, a Crosstab query that lists the names of the employees in rows and each month as a column heading, would be an ideal way to present this type of information.

To create a Crosstab query, open the **ADEPT 1** database and click first the Queries button, then the **New** button on the Database window. Next, select the **Crosstab Query Wizard** option from the list on the New Query dialogue box, as shown on the next page.

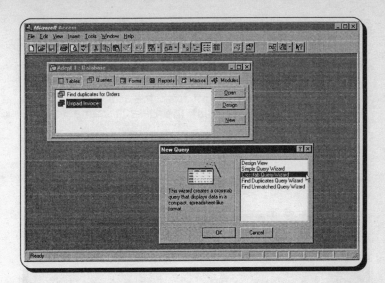

Pressing the **OK** button, causes the Crosstab Query Wizard dialogue box to appear on the screen. Select Orders from the displayed list of tables and press the **Next** button.

From the next dialogue box, select a maximum of three fields from the displayed list, which will become the row

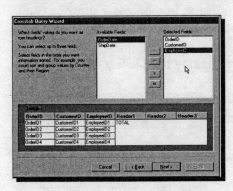

headings of the crosstab form. Choose OrderID, CustomerID, and EmployeeID, in that order, as shown here. The order you select these fields is important as Access will list the results of the query in alphabetical order of the first selected field.

Having selected the three fields, click the **Next** button, and choose the OrderDate as the field whose value you want to be the column headings. Press **Next**, select Month as the time interval by which you want to group your columns and press **Next**. On the following dialogue box choose Count from the Function list and press **Next**. Finally, accept the default name for the query, and press **Finish**.

The result of this Crosstab query are shown below with reduced widths of the monthly columns so that you can see the whole year at a glance.

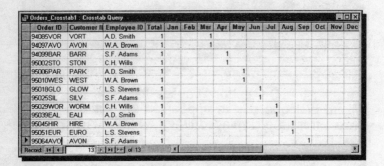

Order ID	Customer I	Employee ID	Total	Jan	Feb	Mar	Apr	May	Jun	Jul	Aug	Sep	Oct	Nov	Dec
94085VOR	VORT	A.D. Smith	1			1									
94097AVO	AVON	W.A. Brown	1		1										
94099BAR	BARR	S.F. Adams	1				1								
95002STO	STON	C.H. Wills	1				1								
95006PAR	PARK	A.D. Smith	1					1							
95010WES	WEST	W.A. Brown	1					1							
95018GLO	GLOW	L.S. Stevens	1						1						
95025SIL	SILV	S.F. Adams	1						1						
95029WOR	WORM	C.H. Wills	1							1					
95039EAL	EALI	A.D. Smith	1							1					
95045HIR	HIRE	W.A. Brown	1								1				
95051EUR	EURO	L.S. Stevens	1								1				
95064AVO	AVON	S.F. Adams	1									1			

As you can see from the above screen, the required information is tabulated and is extremely easy to read. However, the displayed recordset is not updatable.

To see the underlying structure of the query, click the Design View button to display the QBE grid, as follows:

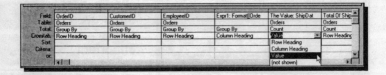

If you want to use a field for grouping, sorting, or setting criteria, but to exclude the field from the recordset, click the arrow in that field's Crosstab cell, and select "(not shown)" from the displayed list.

Creating Queries for Updating Records

When a query is based on either a single table or on two tables with a one-to-one relationship, all the fields in the query are updatable.

Queries which include more than one table, when some of the tables have a one-to-many relationship, are more difficult to design so that they are updatable. Usually, such a query could be designed to be updatable, which is also true of a query that includes an attached table, unless the attached table is a SQL database table with no unique index.

The easiest way of finding out whether you can update records, is to design the query, run it and try to change values in its various fields and also add data. If you can not change values in a field or add data, then you will be warned with an appropriate message on the Status bar.

All other types of queries, such as a Crosstab query, a query with totals, a query with Unique Values property set to Yes, a Union Query, a Pass-through query, a calculated or read-only field, can not be used to update data.

For example, if you try to change the second name under Employee ID from Smith to Smyth, you get the message "This Recordset is not updatable" on the Status bar at the bottom of the screen, shown below.

65

Creating Action Queries

You can create *Action Queries* in the same way as Select Queries. Action Queries are used to make bulk changes to data rather than simply displaying data. For this reason, Action Queries can be dangerous for the novice, simply because they change your database.

There are four different types of Action Queries, with the following functions:

Type of Query	*Function*
Append query	Adds records from one or more tables to another table or tables.
Delete query	Deletes records from a table or tables.
Make-table query	Creates a new table from all or part of another table or tables.
Update query	Changes the data in a group of records

In the previous version of Access, you could quickly create an Action query which moved old orders to an Old Orders Archive table, by using the Archive Query Wizard. A query created by this Wizard will still run quite happily in the new version of Access, but if you want to design such a query from scratch, then you will have to go through the following steps:

- Use the Make-table query to copy selected records from an existing table into a new named, say, Old Orders Archive table.

- Change the design of the Make-table query so that on subsequent execution of the query it Appends selected records from your original table to the Old Orders Archive table.

- Use the Delete query to delete the archived records from the original table.

In what follows, we will go through the steps necessary to create an Old Orders Archive query.

- Open the database **ADEPT 1** and click first the Queries tab, then the **New** button on the Database window.

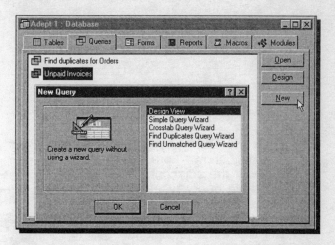

- Select Design View from the displayed list in the New Query dialogue box, shown above, and press **OK**.

- In the Show Table dialogue box that opens next, select Orders, as shown here, then press the **Add** button, followed by the **Close** button. This adds the Orders table to the Select Query window which also contains the QBE grid, so that

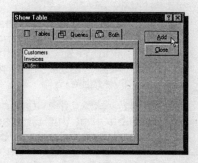

you can design an appropriate query.

- Drag all the fields from the Orders table onto the QBE grid, and add in the OrderDate field the criteria <=4/4/95, as shown below.

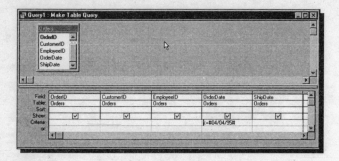

- Click the Query Type button on the Toolbar, shown here, which displays below it the adjacent menu-list of available query types. Select the Make Table option and click the left mouse button which causes the Make Table dialogue box to appear on the screen. Type the name of the new table, say, Old Orders Archive, and press **OK**.

- Press the Run button on the Toolbar, shown here, which causes a warning dialogue box to be displayed. In our example, we are told that three records are about to be appended onto our new table. Pressing **Yes**, copies the selected records from the Orders table to the newly created Old Orders Archive table.

- Next, click the Query Type button on the Toolbar, but this time select the Append option. The Append dialogue box is displayed with the Old Orders Archive name appearing as default. Press **OK** and close the Append Query window.

- On clicking on the 'X' button to close the Append Query window, you will be asked whether you would like your design to be saved. Select **Yes**.

- In the displayed Save As dialogue box, type the new name for the query. We chose to call it Append to Old Orders Archive.

As an exercise, go through the steps of designing the Make Table query, but select the Delete option of the Query Type menu. If you choose to do this, Access places two new queries in the Query list, as shown below. These have an exclamation point attached to their icon so that you don't run them inadvertently.

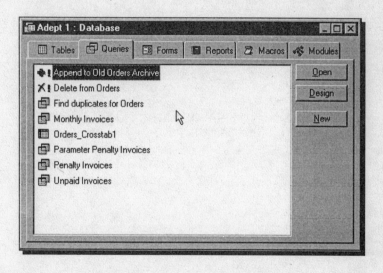

In all, there are four Action queries available in Access. Below we list these, together with their function.

1 The Make-Table query; used to create a table by retrieving the records that meet certain criteria and using them to create a new table.

2 The Append query; used to append (add) records from one table to another existing table.

3   The Update query; used to change data in existing tables, such as the cost per hour charged to your customers.

4   The Delete query; used to delete (remove) records that meet certain pre-defined criteria from a table.

7. USING FORMS & REPORTS

We saw towards the end of Chapter 3 how easy it was to create a single column form to view our Customers table. To see this again, open **ADEPT 1** and in the Database window click the Form tab, then double-click on Form1, which should display the following:

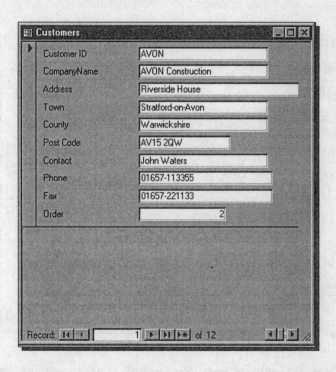

You can use forms to find, edit, and add data in a convenient manner. Access provides you with an easy way of designing various types of forms, some of which are discussed here. Forms look good on screen, but do not produce very good output on paper, whereas reports are designed to look good on paper, but do not necessarily look good on screen.

Using the Form Wizard

Using the Form Wizard, you can easily display data from either a table or a query in form view.

In the Database window, first click the Forms tab, then the **New** button which opens the New Form dialogue box in which you must choose either a table or a query on which to base the new form. In the screen dump below, we have chosen the Invoices table.

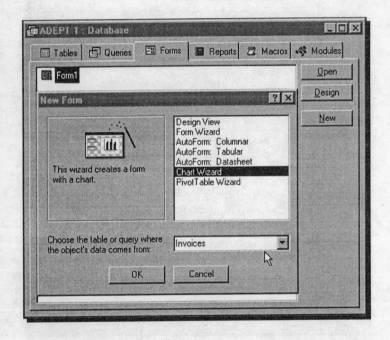

Next, select the **Chart Wizard** option which causes the Form Wizard to display a number of dialogue boxes. As usual, after making appropriate selections, click the **Next** button to progress through the automatic design of the particular form. As you can see from the above screen dump, there are 6 different types of forms available for you to choose from. Their function will be discussed shortly.

72

To continue with our example, the Wizard displays the following dialogue box in which you are asked to specify the fields that contain the data you want to chart. We chose InvoiceID and Amount.

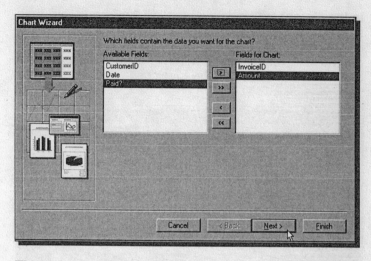

This opens another dialogue box in which you are asked what type of chart you would like. We chose the third one before pressing **Next**.

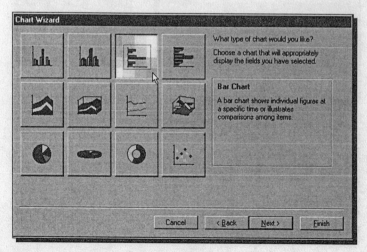

In the following dialogue box, double-click the x-axis button (the one with the caption 'SumOfAmount') and select 'None' from the list in the displayed Summarize dialogue box, shown below, and press **OK**.

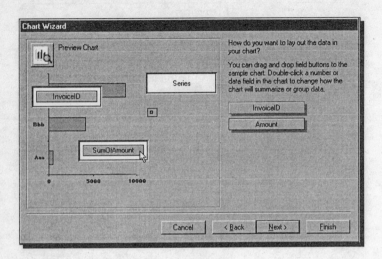

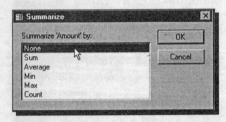

The Wizard then asks you what name you would like to give to this form - we chose to call it 'Invoice Amounts'.

Pressing the **Finish** button, allows the Wizard to display the final result, shown here to the left. It is as easy as that to get a graphical view of the amounts involved in each of your invoices.

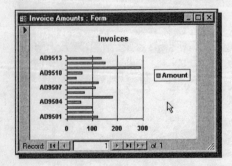

The available choice of Form Wizards have the following function:

Type of Form	Function
Design View	Design a form from scratch.
Form Wizard	Automatically creates a form based on the fields you select.
AutoForm: Columnar	Creates a columnar form with all the field labels appearing in the first column and the data in the second. The form displays one record at a time.
AutoForm: Tabular	Tabulates a screen full of records in tabular form with the field labels appearing at the head of each column.
AutoForm: Datasheet	Similar to the Tabular form, but in worksheet display format.
Chart Wizard	Displays data graphically.
PivotTable Wizard	Creates a form with an Excel PivotTable - an interactive table that can summarise a large number of data using the format and calculation methods specified by the user.

Access also allows you to design a form that contains another form. This type of form, called main/subform, allows data from related tables to be viewed at the same time.

Customising a Form:

You can customise a form by changing the appearance of text, data, and any other attributes. To have a look at some of these options, double click on Form1 to display the Customers form, then click the Design View button on the Toolbar.

What appears on your screen is shown below:

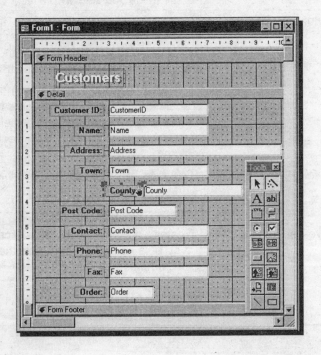

As you can see, a form in Design View is made up of boxes attached to a grid. Clicking at the County box, for example, causes markers to appear around it as shown above. When the mouse pointer is then placed within either the label box or data box, it changes to a hand which indicates that you can drag the box to a new position, as we have done above. This method moves both label and data boxes together.

If you look more closely at the markers around the label and data boxes, you will see that they are of different size, as shown below.

The larger ones are 'move' handles, while the smaller ones are 'size' handles. In the above example you can use the 'move' handles of either the label or the data box to move one independently of the other. The label box can also be sized. To size the data box, click on it so that the markers appear around it.

Boxes on a form can be made larger by simply pointing to the sizing handles and dragging them in the appropriate direction.

In addition to moving and enlarging label and data boxes, you can further customise a form using the various new buttons that appear on the Tool bar when in Design View, shown below in two tiers.

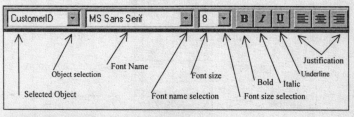

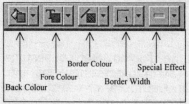 Do try and experiment with moving and sizing label and data boxes and also increasing their font size. If you don't like the result, simply don't save it. Skills gained here will be used in the Report design section.

The Toolbox

The Toolbox can be used either to design a Form or Report from scratch (a task beyond the scope of this book), or to add controls to them, such as a Combo (drop-down) box. The function of each tool on the Toolbox is listed below.

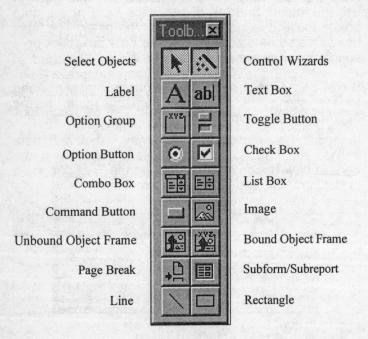

Select Objects	Control Wizards
Label	Text Box
Option Group	Toggle Button
Option Button	Check Box
Combo Box	List Box
Command Button	Image
Unbound Object Frame	Bound Object Frame
Page Break	Subform/Subreport
Line	Rectangle

As an example of using the Toolbox, let us assume that we would like to use a form to enter new data into our Invoices table, but with the ability of selecting the CustomerID field from a drop-down menu - a Combo box.

To achieve the above, execute the following steps:

- On the Database window first click the Forms tab followed by the **New** button.

- In the New Form dialogue box select the **Form Wizard** option, choose Invoices as the table on which to base the new Form, and press the **OK** button.

- In the second dialogue box, select all the fields from the Invoices table, and click the **Next** button.

- In the third dialogue box, select **Columnar** as the preferred form layout, and press **Next**.

- In the fourth dialogue box, select **Standard** as the preferred style for your form and press **Next**.

- In the fifth dialogue box, name your form 'Add Invoices', and press **Finish**. The following form is created and displayed on your screen.

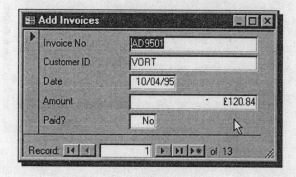

- When the above form appears on the screen, click the Design View button on the Toolbar, and enlarge the Add Invoices form so that both the Header and Footer sections are visible on the form.

- Click the CustomerID field on the form, and delete both its Label and Data boxes by clicking each individually and pressing the <Del> key.

- Click the Combo Box on the Toolbox, and point and click at the area where the CustomerID field used to be on the form.

- In the subsequent dialogue boxes, select options which will cause the Combo Box to look up the values from the Customers table, and from the CustomerID field and store a selected value in the CustomerID field. Specify that the Combo Box should have the label Customer ID:.

- Move and size both the Label and Data boxes of the Combo box into the position shown below.

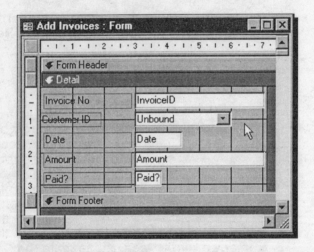

- Click the Form View button on the Toolbar, followed by the New Record button at the bottom of the Add Invoices form, both of which are shown below.

80

* The entry form should now look as follows:

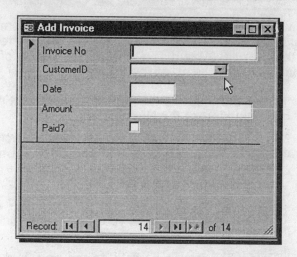

From now on, whenever you want to add a new invoice to the Invoices table, use the Add Invoices form from the Database window, then click the New Record button on either the Toolbar or the Add Invoices form itself to display an empty form. Next, type in the relevant information in the appropriate data boxes on the form, but when you come to fill in the Customer ID field, click instead the down arrow against its data box to display the drop-down menu shown here. Select one of the existing customers on the list, and click the Next Record button at the bottom of the Add Invoices form.

Try the above procedure with the following details:

    AD9514   WEST   28/10/95   £140

then verify that indeed the information has been recorded by double-clicking the Invoices table on the Database window.

Using the Report Wizard

We will use the skills gained in manipulating Forms in Design View to produce an acceptable report created by the Report Wizard. To produce a report of the Unpaid Invoices query, do the following:

- Click the Reports tab on the Database window and then press the **Next** button.

- In the New Report dialogue box, select the **Report Wizard** option, and choose the 'Unpaid Invoices' as the query where the object's data will come from, and press **OK**.

- Select all the fields (except for the Paid? field) which are to appear on your report and click the **Next** button.

- Select the InvoiceID field as the sort field, and accept all subsequent default settings. Call the report 'Unpaid Invoices Report'. The report is created for you as follows:

Unpaid Invoices Report

Invoice No	Order ID	Amount	Name	Contact	Phone
AD9501	94085VOR	£120.84	VORTEX Co. Ltd	Brian Storm	01776-223344
AD9503	94099BAR	£99.32	BARROWS Associ	Mandy Brown	01554-664422
AD9504	95002STO	£55.98	STONEAGE Ltd	Mike Irons	01765-234567
AD9505	95006PAR	£180.22	PARKWAY Gravel	James Stone	01534-987654
AD9506	95010WES	£68.52	WESTWOOD Ltd	Mary Slim	01234-667755
AD9507	95018GLO	£111.56	GLOWORM Ltd	Peter Summers	01432-746523
AD9509	95029WOR	£35.87	WORMGLAZE Ltd	Richard Glazer	01123-654321
AD9510	95039EAL	£58.95	EALING Engines D	Trevor Miles	01336-010107
AD9511	95045HIR	£290.00	HIRE Service Equi	Nicole Webb	01875-558822
AD9512	95051EUR	£150.00	EUROBASE Co. Lt	Sarah Star	01736-098765
AD9513	94097AVO	£135.00	AVON Constructio	John Waters	01657-113355
AD9513	95064AVO	£135.00	AVON Constructio	John Waters	01657-113355

Obviously this report is not quite acceptable. The problem is mainly the fact that all text fields are left justified within their columns, while numerical fields are right justified.

What we need to do is display it in Design View so that we can change the position of the numeric fields. To do

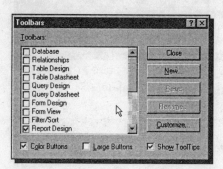

this, use the **View, Toolbars** command, highlight the Report Design item in the **Toolbars** list of the displayed dialogue box, shown here, and press the **Close** button. This displays an additional Toolbar which allows you access to the Design View button. Clicking this button displays the Report as follows:

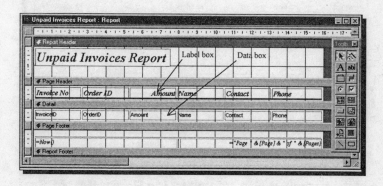

Use the mouse to move the Amount data box to the left, and then right justify the text in the Amount label and data boxes and make them smaller, as shown on the next page.

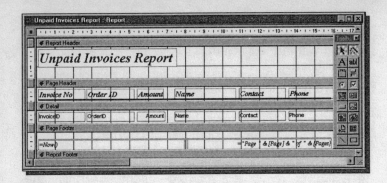

The corresponding report is now as follows:

Unpaid Invoices Report

Invoice No	Order ID	Amount	Name	Contact	Phone
AD9501	94085VOR	£120.84	VORTEX Co. Ltd	Brian Storm	01776-223344
AD9503	94099BAR	£99.32	BARROWS Associates	Mandy Brown	01554-664422
AD9504	95002STO	£55.98	STONEAGE Ltd	Mike Irons	01765-234567
AD9505	95006PAR	£180.22	PARKWAY Gravel	James Stone	01534-987654
AD9506	95010WES	£68.52	WESTWOOD Ltd	Mary Slim	01234-667755
AD9507	95018GLO	£111.56	GLOWORM Ltd	Peter Summers	01432-746523
AD9509	95029WOR	£35.87	WORMGLAZE Ltd	Richard Glazer	01123-654321
AD9510	95039EAL	£58.95	EALING Engines Design	Trevor Miles	01336-010107
AD9511	9504SHIR	£290.00	HIRE Service Equipment	Nicole Webb	01875-558822
AD9512	95051EUR	£150.00	EUROBASE Co. Ltd	Sarah Star	01736-098765
AD9513	94097AVO	£135.00	AVON Construction	John Waters	01657-113355
AD9513	95064AVO	£135.00	AVON Construction	John Waters	01657-113355

This layout is obviously far more acceptable than that of the original report created by the Report Wizard.

8. MASKING AND FILTERING DATA

In this chapter we discuss two aspects of working with data; masking and filtering. The first is useful for restricting data input into an Access field, such as a postcode or a telephone number, to a given data mask so as to eliminate input errors. The second is invaluable if you are thinking of importing data into Access either from a flat-file database or spreadsheet, or exporting data from Access into another Windows package, such as Microsoft Word or Excel.

The InputMask Property

You can use the InputMask property to make data entry easier and control the values you enter in a text box. For example, you could create an input mask for a Post Code field that shows you exactly how to enter a new postcode.

To see an input mask, open the **ADEPT 1** database, select the Customers table, press the **Design** button, and select the Post Code field. The input mask appears in the Field Properties box, shown below.

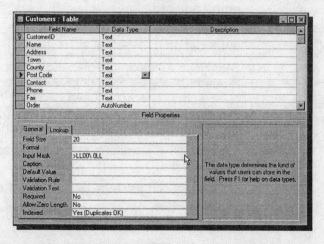

The InputMask property can contain up to three sections separated by semicolons (;). Within each section a certain number of characters are allowed. These characters and their description are listed below.

Character   *Description*

0	Signifies a digit (0 to 9); entry required. The plus (+) and minus (-) signs are not allowed.
9	Signifies a digit or space; entry not required. The plus and minus signs are not allowed.
#	Signifies a digit or space; entry not required, spaces are displayed as blanks while in Edit mode, but blanks are removed when data is saved. The plus and minus signs are allowed.
L	Signifies a letter (A to Z); entry required.
?	Signifies a letter (A to Z); entry optional.
A	Signifies a letter or digit; entry required.
a	Signifies a letter or digit; entry optional.
&	Signifies any character or a space; entry required.
C	Signifies any character or a space; entry optional.
. , : ; - /	Signifies a decimal placeholder and thousand, date, and time separators. (The actual character used depends on the settings in the Regional Settings section of the Windows Control Panel).
<	Causes all characters to be converted to lowercase.
>	Causes all characters to be converted to uppercase.

!	Causes the input mask to display from right to left, rather than from left to right, when characters on the left side of the input mask are optional. Characters typed into the mask always fill it from left to right. You can include the exclamation point anywhere in the input mask.
\	Causes the character that follows to be displayed as the literal character (for example, \A is displayed as just A).

Thus, we can interpret the postcode shown in our earlier screen dump as follows:

>	Convert all characters entered to upper case.
L	Letter (A-Z) expected; entry required.
L	Letter (A-Z) expected; entry required.
0	Digit (0-9) expected; entry required.
0	Digit (0-9) expected; entry required.
\	Cause character following backslash (in this case a space) to appear as such
0	Digit (0-9) expected; entry required.
L	Letter (A-Z) expected; entry required.
L	Letter (A-Z) expected; entry required.

However, this postcode (two letters followed by two numbers, then a space followed by one number, then two letters, will not be adequate enough for all the variation of postcode encountered.

For example, some codes have only one number following the first two letters, like CB1 2PU, others particularly in London have only one leading letter, like N1 0RD, while if you write to the BBC you will need the W1A 1AA code.

Thus a postcode mask suitable for most eventualities in the UK could be:

    >LAa&\ 0LL

To experiment with input masks, place the insertion pointer in the Post Code field of the Customers table. This causes a dotted button to appear at the extreme right of the field which, when clicked, activates the Input Mask Wizard, as shown below.

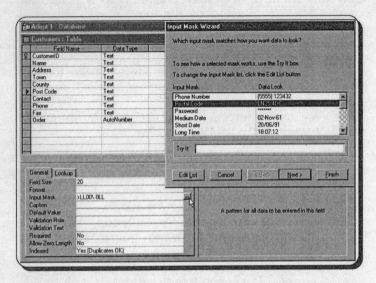

Select the Post Code from the Input Mask list, and press **Next** to display the second dialogue box in which you can edit the default Input Mask. You can also type the variations of the postcode in the Try It box.

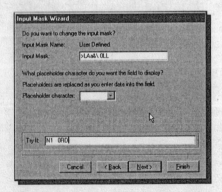

Always place the insertion pointer at the extreme left of the Try It box, and provide one space between the two sections of the postcode (two if the first section has only 2 characters. Can you think of a better input mask?

88

Note: If you want to create a password-entry control, use the Password input mask to set the InputMask property to the word 'Password'. This displays an asterisk (*) on the screen for every typed character.

Only characters that you type directly in a control or combo box are affected by the input mask. Microsoft Access ignores any input masks when you import data, or run an action query.

If you define an input mask and also set the Format property for the same field, the Format property takes precedence when the data is displayed. The data in the underlying table itself is not changed, but the Format property affects the way it is displayed.

The three sections of an input mask and their description are listed below.

Section	*Description*
First	Specifies the input mask itself, for example, >LL00\ 0LL or (0171) 553344.
Second	Specifies whether Microsoft Access stores the literal display characters in the table when you enter data. If you use 0 for this section, all literal display characters (for example, the parentheses in a phone number input mask) are stored with the value; if you enter 1 or leave this section blank, only characters typed into the control are stored.
Third	Specifies the character that Microsoft Access displays for the space where you should type a character in the input mask. For this section, you can use any character; to display an empty string, use a space enclosed in quotation marks (" ").

The Input Mask Wizard will set the property for you.

Importing or Linking Data

Microsoft Access has an extensive help topic on importing and linking data created in other programs. Below we present the most important parts of this information so as to make it easy for you to follow.

Access can import or link table data from other Access databases (version 1.x, 2.0, and 7.0), as well as data from other programs and file formats, such as Excel, dBASE, FoxPro, or Paradox. Importing data creates a copy of the information in a new table in your current Access database; the source table or file is not altered. Linking data allows you to read and update data in the external data source without importing; the external data source's format is not altered so that you can continue to use the file with the program that created it originally, and you can also add, delete, or edit such data using Access.

In general, you import or link information depending on the imposed situation, as follows:

Imposed Situation	Method to Adopt
Inserted data needs to be updated in Access as changes are made to the data in the source file, or Source file will always be available and you want to minimise the size of the Access data file.	Link
Inserted information might need to be updated but source file might not be always accessible, or Access data file needs to be edited without having these changes reflected in the source file.	Import

However, to import or link data, you must create or open an Access database to contain the information.

If you have data in any of the following programs or formats, you can either import or link such files.

Data source	Version or Format
Excel spreadsheets	2.0, 3.0, 4.0, 5.0, and 7.0
Lotus 1-2-3 spreadsheets	.WKS, .WK1, and .WK3
dBASE	III, III+, IV, and 5
FoxPro	2.0, 2.5, 2.6, and 3.0 (import only)
Paradox	3.x, 4.x, and 5.0
Delimited text files	Most files with values separated by commas, tabs, or other characters; must be in MS-DOS or Windows ANSI text format
Fixed-width text files	Most files with values arranged so that each field has a certain width; must be in MS-DOS or Windows ANSI text format

If you have a program whose data is not stored in one of the above formats, but the program can export, convert, or save its data as one of these formats, you can import that data as well.

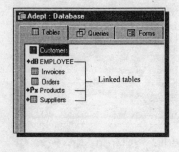

Microsoft Access uses different icons to represent linked tables and tables that are stored in the current database, as shown here. The icon that represents a linked table remains in the Database window along with tables in the current database, so you can open the table whenever you want.

Microsoft Access displays a different icon for tables from each type of source database. If you delete the icon for a linked table, you delete the link to the table, not the external table itself.

When importing data, you cannot append data to existing tables (except when importing spreadsheet or text files). However, once you have imported a table, you can use an append query to add its data to another table.

You can also import database objects other than tables, such as forms or reports, from another Access database. When importing such objects from another Access database, you can choose to import all, or just a subset of those objects, in a single operation.

When you link or embed an object, such as a ClipArt image or an image you've scanned and saved, in a Microsoft Access form or report, the object is displayed in an object frame. To illustrate this point, start Access, select the Forms tab, and open Form1, which we created in Chapter 3. Then do the following:

- Switch to Design View, then use the **Insert, Object** command which displays the Insert Object dialogue box.

- Select the source application from the **Object Type** list (we have selected the Microsoft ClipArt Gallery), and press **OK**.

- Select the object and press **Insert**. This inserts the object into an unbound frame.

If the object you are embedding is from an Access table, use a bound object frame.

Converting Data to Microsoft Access

If you have been using Microsoft Excel, another spreadsheet, or a flat-file database to keep an invoicing list, you will soon run out of disc space, as such lists include repeated data, such as the address information on invoices issued to the same firm.

Converting a list from Excel to Access is extremely easy; simply start Excel, open the workbook that contains your list, then use the **Data, Convert To Access** command. From that point on, an Access wizard takes over and steps you through the process of conversion, which will be discussed shortly.

Converting a list from another spreadsheet or a flat-file database, whose format cannot be read by Excel, you will need to use the original package to save the list in ASCII format. To illustrate the point, we will step through the conversion process, using data that were originally created in a flat-file database. The type of information held in this database was as follows:

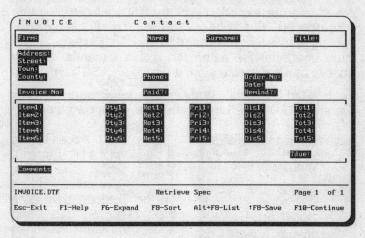

Your database is bound to be different. In what follows, it would be beneficial to you if you could use your own flat-file database data while following our example.

First, we used the package's export facility to convert and save the data into ASCII delimited format, with quotes around text values and fields separated by a comma. Our package displayed the screen below. Yours, of course, might display a different screen.

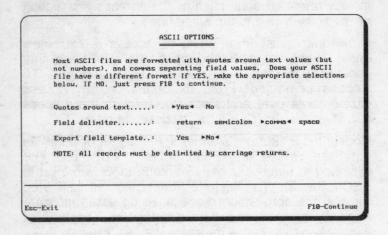

```
                        ASCII OPTIONS

     Most ASCII files are formatted with quotes around text values (but
     not numbers), and commas separating field values. Does your ASCII
     file have a different format? If YES, make the appropriate selections
     below. If NO, just press F10 to continue.


     Quotes around text.....:    ►Yes◄  No

     Field delimiter........:    return  semicolon ►comma◄ space

     Export field template..:    Yes  ►No◄

     NOTE: All records must be delimited by carriage returns.



Esc-Exit                                              F10-Continue
```

We saved the exported ASCII file under the filename **Invoicdb.txt** (we choose here the 8.3 character naming convention demanded by the package). The three character file extension **.txt** is essential so that Access can recognise such a file as an ASCII type.

Next, start Access, and select to Create a New Database Using a **Blank Database**, as shown below.

 If Access is already running, click the New Database button on the Toolbar, then click the General tab and accept the blank database design. Pressing **OK**, displays the File New Database dialogue box, shown on the next page.

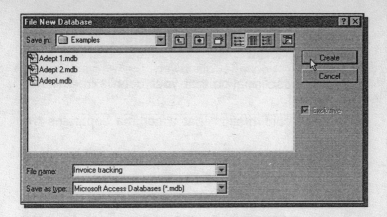

In the **File name** box type the name 'Invoice tracking', and in the **Save in** box specify the folder in which you would like to save your database (we chose the Access\Examples folder) and press the **Create** button.

When the new database window appears, use the **File, Get External Data, Import** command. In the displayed Import window, select Text Files in the **Files of type** box and instruct Access to **Look in** the drive and folder you have saved the **invoicdb.txt** file, as shown below.

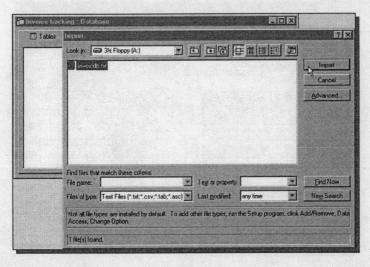

From this point on, the Text Import Wizard takes over by displaying a succession of dialogue boxes. Their function is as follows:

1. Asks confirmation that your data is in delimited format.

2. Asks confirmation that a comma separates the fields.

3. Asks confirmation that you would like to store the data in a new table.

4. Asks what you want to call the various fields in the imported table (see below). Each field can be selected by clicking its name. Take the opportunity at this point to expand or change the name of the original fields so that they are easier to identify, but make sure to use the underscore to separate words and don't include full stops. Also, for each **Field Name**, click the down arrow button against the **Data Type** box to select its data type. This is by far the most time consuming part of the whole importing process.

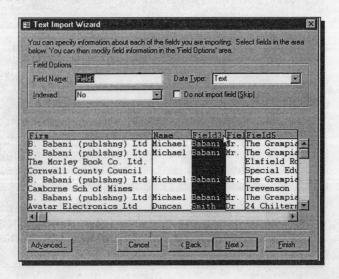

5. Asks for confirmation on allowing Access to choose the Primary Key.

6. Asks for confirmation on the name of the table in which to import your data, as shown below. In this dialogue box, check the **I would like a wizard to analyze my table after importing the data** box, before pressing the **Finish** button.

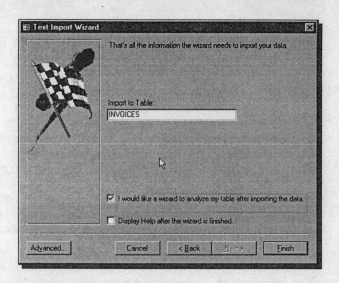

7. Importing is completed and the wizard asks confirmation on whether to start analysing your data.

The Table Analyzer Wizard:

From this point on, the Table Analyzer Wizard starts looking at your data trying to find duplicate information and the possibility of spitting the table so that each piece of information is only stored once.

We suggest that you decide which fields go into which table. For example, the first nine fields of our chosen database holds information on our customer's name and address which makes them ideal for selection.

Select such fields that hold common information and drag them on the working area of the wizard's window. Table2 is immediately formed and you are asked to name it. We called ours 'Customers', as shown below.

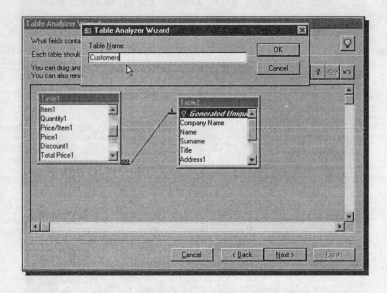

In the next dialogue box, the Table Analyzer Wizard presents you with records that it thinks might be similar to others, but for slight differences. For example, you might have abbreviated a firm's name differently, or placed address elements at different fields. It is at this point that you have the chance to correct the original.

Select each disputed record in turn and click the down arrow button in the **Correct** column of the window, as shown on the next page. This reveals a list of records that the wizard thinks are similar to the selected one. You can either associate the selected record with one on the displayed list by highlighting it and clicking, or you can select the 'Leave as it is' option, if the selected record is indeed different from those in the list.

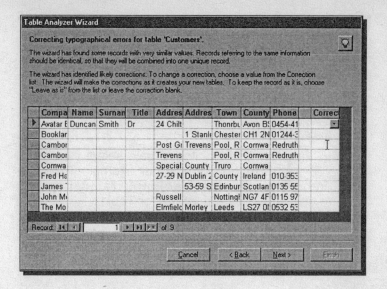

Finally, the Table Analyzer Wizard displays its last dialogue box. Make sure you select the **Yes, create the query** option, as shown below.

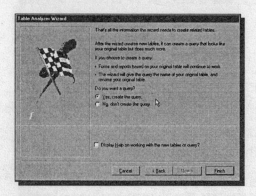

This option builds a query that looks like your original imported data file, but also includes extra capabilities.

For example, changing a repeating entry in one place, updates every affected record and when you enter a new firm's name, in a new record, Access assigns it a new, unique, ID automatically.

Rebuilding Formulae to Calculate Values:

When you export your data, formulae in the original database or spreadsheet are lost. Such formulae are best rebuilt within a database form, as follows:

- In the Database window, click the Form tab and then the **New** button to open the New Form dialogue box.

- In the New Form dialogue box, select the table you want to work with (in our example Table1), and double-click the **AutoForm: Tabular** option to display a data entry form for Table1.

- Click the Form View icon on the Toolbar to select the Design View option and rearrange the various fields in the form to your liking. We rearrange ours as shown below.

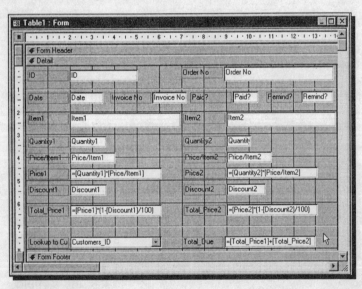

As you can see, we have only imported enough fields to deal with two categories of items, Item1 and Item2. The original database had five categories of items.

- In our example, formulae were inserted in the listed fields below, by double-clicking the data part of each field in our form in Design View and replacing what was displayed there with our formula. These changes are also shown on the screen dump of the previous page.

Field	Formula used
Price1	=[Quantity1]*[Price/Item1]
Total_Price1	=[Price1]*(1-[Discount1]/100)
Price2	=[Quantity2]*[Price/Item2]
Total_Price2	=[Price2]*(1-[Discount2]/100)
Total_Due	=[Total_Price1]+[Total_Price2]

The data values of these fields were also formatted to currency, as explained below.

While in Design View, point and left-click on the data part of a given field to select it. Then right-click this field to reveal the shortcut menu shown here. Select the **Properties** option and left-click to display the properties of the selected Text Box.

As you can see, the formula you typed in the data box of the field, appears as an entry in the Control Source section of the All tab of the Text Box. To format data in a field, click against the Format entry and select from the displayed list.

101

* * * * *

Access for Windows 95 is capable of a lot more than what we were able to cover in the space allocated to this short book. However, we hope we have covered enough features of the program to make you want to explore Microsoft Access more fully in you own time.

* * * * *

9. GLOSSARY OF TERMS

Application

Software (program) designed to carry out certain activity, such as Access's ability to manage information.

ASCII

A binary code representation of a character set. The name stands for 'American Standard Code for Information Interchange'.

Bitmap

A technique for managing the image displayed on a computer screen.

Browse

A button in some dialogue boxes that lets you view a list of files and folders before you make a selection.

CD-ROM

A device which when installed on your PC, allows the use of CDs.

Check box

A small box in a dialogue box that can be selected (✓), or cleared (empty).

Click

To quickly press and release a mouse button.

Client application

A Windows application that can accept linked, or embedded, objects.

Clipboard

A temporary storage area of memory, where text and graphics are stored with the cut and copy actions.

Close	To remove a dialogue box or window, or to exit a program.
Command	An instruction given to a computer to carry out a particular action.
CPU	The Central Processing Unit; the main chip that executes all instructions entered into a computer.
Cursor	The blinking line indicating where the next input can be entered.
Database	A collection of related information or data, organised for a specific theme in one or more tables.
DDE	Dynamic data exchange - a process that enables you to exchange data between two or more Windows programs.
Default	The command, device or option automatically chosen by the system.
Dialogue box	A window displayed on the screen to allow the user to enter information.
Dimmed	Unavailable menu options shown in a different colour.
Disc	A device on which you can store programs and data.
Disc file	A collection of program code, or data, that is stored under a given name on a disc.

Document	A file produced by an application program.
Double-click	To quickly press and release a mouse button twice.
DPI	Dots Per Inch; a resolution standard for laser printers.
Drag	To press and hold down the left mouse button while moving the mouse, to move an object on the screen.
Drive name	The letter (followed by a colon) which identifies a floppy disc drive, a hard disc drive, or a CD-ROM drive.
Embedded object	Information in a document that is 'copied' from its source application. Selecting the object opens the creating application from within the document.
Field	A single column of information of the same type.
File	The name given to an area on disc containing a program or data.
File extension	The optional three-letter suffix following the period in a filename. Windows 95 uses the extension to identify the filetype.
Filename	The name given to a file. In Windows 95 this can be up to 255 characters long.
Filespec	File specification made up of drive, path and filename.

Fixed disc	The hard disc of a computer.
Floppy disc	A removable disc on which information can be stored magnetically. The two main types are a 5¼" flexible disc, and a 3½" stiff disc.
Folder	An area on disc where information relating to a group of files is kept.
Font	A graphic design representing a set of characters, numbers and symbols.
Formatting	The process of preparing a disc so that it can store information.
Function	A built-in formula which performs specific calculations in a spreadsheet or database cell.
Function key	One of the series of 10 or 12 keys marked with the letter F and a numeral, used for specific operations.
Hardcopy	Output on paper.
Hard disc	A device built into the computer for holding programs and data. It is sometimes referred to as a fixed disc.
Hardware	The equipment that makes up a computer system, excluding the programs or software.
Help	A Windows system that gives you instructions and additional information.

Highlight	The change to a reverse-video appearance when a menu item or area of text is selected.
Icon	A small graphic image that represents a function or object. Clicking on an icon produces an action.
Insertion point	A flashing bar that shows where typed text will be entered into a document.
Kilobyte	(KB); 1024 bytes of information or storage space.
LAN	Local Area Network; PCs, workstations or minis sharing files and peripherals within the same site.
Linked object	A placeholder for an object inserted into a destination document.
Local	A resource that is located on your computer, not linked to it over a network.
Log on	To gain access to a network.
Long filename	In Windows 95 the name given to a file can be up to 255 characters long.
MCI	Media Control Interface - a standard for files and multimedia devices.
Megabyte	(MB); 1024 kilobytes of information or storage space.

Megahertz	(MHz); Speed of processor in millions of cycles per second.
Memory	Part of computer consisting of storage elements organised into addressable locations that can hold data and instructions.
Menu	A list of available options in an application.
Menu bar	The horizontal bar that lists the names of menus.
Microprocessor	The calculating chip within a computer.
Monitor	The display device connected to your PC.
Mouse	A device used to manipulate a pointer around your display and activate a certain process by pressing a button.
Network server	Central computer which stores files for several linked computers.
Password	A unique character string used to gain access to a network, or an application document.
PATH	The location of a file in the directory tree.
PCX	A standard file format used for bitmapped graphics.
Peripheral	Any device attached to a PC.

Pixel	A picture element on screen; the smallest element that can be independently assigned colour and intensity.
Port	An input/output address through which your PC interacts with external devices.
Program	A set of instructions which cause the computer to perform certain tasks.
Protocol	It defines the way in which data is transferred over a network.
Processor	The electronic device which performs calculations.
RAM	Random Access Memory. The micro's volatile memory. Data held in it is lost when power is switched off.
Record	A row of information in a table relating to a single entry and comprising one or more fields.
Resource	A directory, or printer, that can be shared over a network.
ROM	Read Only Memory. A PC's non-volatile memory. Data is written into this memory at manufacture and is not affected by power loss.
Scroll bar	A bar that appears at the right side or bottom edge of a window.

Server	A networked computer that is used to share resources.
Shared resource	Any device, program or file that is available to network users.
Software	The programs and instructions that control your PC.
Spreadsheet	An electronic page made of a matrix of rows and columns.
SVGA	Super Video Graphics Array; it has all the VGA modes but with 256 colours.
Template	A file blank you can create to contain common text and formatting to use as a basis for new documents.
Text file	An unformatted file of text characters saved in ASCII format.
Toolbar	A bar containing icons giving quick access to commands.
Toggle	To turn an action on and off with the same switch.
TrueType fonts	Fonts that can be scaled to any size and print as they show on the screen.
VGA	Video Graphics Array; has all modes of EGA, but with 16 colours.
Wildcard character	A character that can be included in a filename to indicate any other character (?) or group of characters (*).

INDEX

A

Access screen 8
Action queries 43, 66
Active window 8
Adding
   fields to queries 46
   records 28
   tables 31, 39, 57
AND criteria 49
Advanced queries 57
Append query 66
Application control menu . 8

B

Buttons 7

C

Calculated fields 52
Calculating query totals . 55
Closing a window 9
Combining criteria 49
Context sensitive help ... 18
Control Panel 4
Converting data 93
Creating
   calculated fields 52
   queries 41
   tables 21, 39
Criteria
   AND 49
   OR 50
   types 48
Crosstab query 43, 62
Customising forms 76

D

Data-definition query 43
Database
   basics 19
   definition 1
   elements 19
   flat-file 2
   form 27, 71
   management system .. 1
   open dialogue box ... 16
   relationships 37
   size 1
   table 21
   Wizard 19
Delete query 66
Deleting
   fields 29
   records 29
Design
   table 21
   view 23
Dialogue boxes 16

E

Edit command 12
Editing relationships 37
Equi-joins 59
Export data 93

F

Field
   definition 1
   names 22
File command 11, 12
Filename extensions 20, 94
Filtering data 26, 85

Finding
    duplicate records 41
    part of data field 55
    part of text field 54
    records 28
Flat file 2
Form
    customising 76
    types 72
    Wizard 72
Forms 20, 27, 71
Functions in criteria 54

H
Hardware requirements .. 3
Help command 13, 17

I
Icons 7
Importing data 90
Inherited relationships ... 37
Inner joins 59
Input mask property 85
Insert command 13
Inserting
    fields 29
    objects 92
Installing Access 4

J
Joins 35, 59

L
Linking data 90

M
Make-table query 66
Masking data 85
Maximise button 9

Maximum
    fields in a table 1
    objects in database ... 1
Menu
    bar 8, 10
    bar options 11
Minimise button 8, 9
Mouse pointer(s) 8, 14
Moving fields 29

N
New
    database 19
    query 45

O
Office shortcut bar 6
On-line help 18
Opening documents 16
Operating system 3
OR criteria 50
Outer joins 59

P
Parameter query 60
Pass-through query 43
Printing tables 30

Q
QBE grid 43
Queries 20, 41
Query
    action 66
    crosstab 62
    parameter 60
    totals 55
    types 43
    updating 65
    window 44
    Wizard 45

R

RAM 3
Rebuilding formulae 100
Record definition 1
Redesigning a Table 23
Referential integrity 37
Relational database .. 1, 31
Relationships 35
Report Wizard 82
Reports 20, 71
Restore button 8, 9

S

Scroll
    bar 8, 10
    button 8, 10
Select query 42
Self-joins 59
Setup program 4
Shortcut menus 16
Software requirement 3
Sort filter 26
Sorting a Table 25
Starting Access 7
Status bar 8, 10
Start button 4
SQL statements 43, 44

T

Table
    definition 1
    design 21
    view printing 30
    Wizard 21
Title bar 8, 9
Tool bar 8, 10
Tools command 13
Toolbox 78
Totals in queries 55

Types of
    criteria 48
    forms 72
    joins 35, 59
    queries 43
    relationships 37

U

Union query 43
Update query 65, 66
Using
    Form Wizard 72
    forms 27, 71
    functions in criteria ... 54
    help 17
    parameter query 60
    Query Wizard 45
    Report Wizard 82
    reports 71
    Table Analyzer Wizard 97
    Table Wizard 21
    wildcard characters .. 48

V

View command 12
Viewing relationships 37

W

Wildcard characters 48
Window command 13
Windows program 3
Wizards
    Form 72
    Query 45
    Report 82
    Table 21
    Table Analyzer 97

NOTES

COMPANION DISCS TO BOOKS

COMPANION DISCS are available for most books written by the same author(s) and published by BERNARD BABANI (publishing) LTD, as listed at the front of this book (except for those marked with an asterisk). These books contain many pages of file/program listings. There is no reason why you should spend hours typing them into your computer, unless you wish to do so, or need the practice.

COMPANION DISCS come in 3½" format with all example listings.

ORDERING INSTRUCTIONS

To obtain your copy of a companion disc, fill in the order form below or a copy of it, enclose a cheque (payable to **P.R.M. Oliver**) or a postal order, and send it to the address below. Make sure you fill in your name and address and specify the book number and title in your order.

Book No.	Book Name	Unit Price	Total Price
BP		£3.50	
BP		£3.50	
BP		£3.50	
Name .... Address:		Sub-total	£.............
		P & P (@ 45p/disc)	£.............
		Total Due	£.............
Send to: P.R.M. Oliver, CSM, Pool, Redruth, Cornwall, TR15 3SE			

PLEASE NOTE

The author(s) are fully responsible for providing this Companion Disc service. The publishers of this book accept no responsibility for the supply, quality, or magnetic contents of the disc, or in respect of any damage, or injury that might be suffered or caused by its use.